HANG LOOSE WITHOUT BOOZE

81 Simple Tools to Stress Less & Relax More Without Drinking Alcohol

BY
KEVIN O'HARA

A UNIQUE, FREE, ONLINE QUIT-ALCOHOL RESOURCE
VISIT: ALCOHOLMASTERY.COM

themselves, not affiliated with this document.

The information contained on this book, is meant to serve as a collection of facts that have been compiled to educate the reader. It is not intended to be a substitute for professional advice and a professional should always be consulted. The author has made all reasonable efforts to provide current and accurate information for the readers of this information and will not be held liable for any unintentional errors or omissions that may be found. If there is a disagreement between the information in this book and what a professional has told you, it is more likely that the professional is correct. They have the benefit of knowing you and your situation.

This book and the information contained within is for entertainment purposes only. The views expressed are those of the author alone, and should not be taken as expert instruction or commands. The reader is responsible for his or her own actions. Neither the author nor the publisher assumes any responsibility or liability whatsoever on the behalf of the purchaser or reader of these materials. Any perceived slight of any individual or organization is purely unintentional.

First edition, 2015

ISBN-13: 978-1519484987

ISBN-10: 1519484984

The Challenge of Quitting Drinking

"I suppose it is tempting, if the only tool you have is a hammer, to treat everything as if it were a nail."

Abraham Maslow

Hang Loose Without Booze is a collection of creative, legal, healthy, and playful ways to find natural highs in your life. These dynamic tools will help you to feel naturally relaxed and stress free, without harming yourself with alcohol and other drugs.

How to Use This Book?

There are far better ways of relaxing, dealing with stress, or getting to sleep at night other than contaminating your body with the toxins contained in alcohol or other drugs.

Although you might find short-term relief in drinking alcohol, it comes at the cost of physical and mental retardation. The easy-to-implement 'highs' you'll find in *Hang Loose Without Booze* will instead help you to take control of your moods and emotions in a positive, healthy, and sustainable manner.

These are tools that you can **use immediately**. When you feel stressed or tense, choose one of the methods outlined and just do it, it's as simple as that. Some of the methods will deliver immediate results, others require a little practice and patience before you feel the benefits.

These are tools that **put YOU in control**. Seeking stress relief or relaxation in any drug hands control of your emotions to an outside force, a force that can have deadly consequences. You don't have to do that. Learning a few simple techniques and skills is all it takes to harness your own powerful natural capacities for stress management and relaxation.

These tools are **free or relatively inexpensive**. Most of us are on a budget, with both our time and money. It's just not possible for us to take multiple vacations, visits to the local spa, or health retreats. The aim of this book is to introduce small changes into your life on a day-to-day basis. These small changes won't cost you anything, for the most part, but with practice they'll bring you an abundance of serenity and calmness. They will also give you mental and physical stability and confidence in your own abilities to conquer any issue that may arise in your life.

Who is This Book For?

Although the book is primarily aimed at people who're looking for an alternative to drugs, particularly alcohol, the contents can be used by anyone who wants really effective and healthy ways of relaxing and managing stress without killing themselves in the process.

I've adopted many of these suggestions into my own life. For instance, I'm a big fan of walking, forest bathing, yoga, and the 7 minute workout. I'm also a huge believer that what you put into your body is the single most important change that you can make in your life. That's why I've devoted such a large chunk of this information to talking about nutrition.

You are what you eat might be a cliche, but it's still very true. The food you eat gives you the fuel you need for your day-to-day living. Food is also the basic building block of who you are, literally. **What you eat becomes the future you!**

Let's take a couple of examples. Your taste buds are replaced every 10 days. Certain parts of your lungs are only 3 weeks old. You grow a new outer-skin every 28 days. You grow a new liver every 5 months. Your entire skeleton is replaced every 10 years.

How does your body do this?

The answer is through the food you eat. The food you put into your body today is going to become the material that your future self is built on. Your present body is constructed of what you've eaten in the past. A junk food diet provides junk building blocks. Junk building blocks make junk skin, junk lungs, a junk liver, and a junk skeleton. Junk food feeds the brain with junk fuel which can only ever lead to junk thoughts.

A diet high in nutrients, on the other hand, provides high quality building blocks. High quality building blocks builds a high quality body. High quality brain food produces high quality thinking, leading to better decision-making, stamina, and self-control.

It's as simple as that.

This principle also applies to how you feel, to your emotional stability, and how you deal with life. A huge part of your emotional well-being depends on eating the right foods and avoiding the crap, drinking the right drinks and avoiding the crap.

If you're looking for **one area in your life which will give you the biggest bang for your buck**, careful and planned nutrition should be it. If the only part of this book you implement is to change what you put into your body, it will be the biggest single step you can take towards feeling 100% more alive. Good nutrition is your best medicine for relaxing and handling any problems that your life can throw at you, moving yourself onwards and upwards toward the person you would like to become.

Just as a new house is built one block at a time, so a new life is built one skill at a time. Leaving alcohol in your past and moving towards the new you requires that you learn new skills or relearn old ones. Some of the most valuable skills you can learn are how to relax and deal with your stress without drugs. When you can do this in a positive enervating way, you build the strength and willpower you need to make all the other necessary changes in your life.

About Me

My name is Kevin O'Hara and I run the website AlcoholMastery.com.

The aim of AlcoholMastery.com is to provide a place where alcohol users can see that most problems with their alcohol use are down to habit rather than alcoholism. Alcoholism is just a convenient one-fits-all term used by people to cover up the real issues about how alcohol is used in our society.

What I show you, through simple easy to apply strategies, is that you really are in control of your alcohol drinking and of your not-drinking. Quitting alcohol doesn't have to be a terrible experience. In fact, stopping drinking this toxin is the best thing you can ever do for your life and for the lives of your family and friends.

1. Food Stress Builders and Food Stress Busters

You Are What You Eat

The reason I've devoted a lot of this book to nutrition is because I believe that taking care about what you put into your body is the best way of optimizing your health into the future. What you eat or drink has a direct influence on how you feel in your mind and your body. There's a lot of truth in the statement 'you are what you eat'! If you want to feel good, eat good food. If you want to feel like crap, eat crappy food.

Most of the processed and packaged foods you are likely to find in your local supermarket will not give you the best nutrition, some won't give you any nutrition at all.

The mass-production techniques which are used in food processing put massive pressure on the base raw materials. Any food that goes through these industrial processes loses a large percentage of its natural vitamins and minerals. What nutrients that are left after the initial processing are further corrupted as the food sits around at room temperatures in warehouses, in the backs of trucks, in storerooms, and sitting on the shelves of your local supermarket for weeks, and sometimes months or years. Ultimately, when you bring this food home (can you call it food at this stage), it has to be cooked or heated which wipes out more nutrients.

In order for these products to sit around for weeks or months on end, without going rancid, the manufacturers must to adulterate them with additives, usually chemical additives. These artificial preservatives, flavorings, and colorings are there to fool you into believing that the product is 'fresh'.

As you quit drinking alcohol, you need to do as much as you can to help your body overcome the toxins that you have swallowed over all your years of boozing. Don't add to that intoxication by eating junk food.

Over the next few sections, we're going to take a quick look at where you can make better food and drink choices. Then we'll look at some of the foods and drinks to avoid and which foods are likely to help you relax and feel less stressed out.

2. Emotional Eating - Food is Fuel NOT Therapy!

Before we start looking at the types of foods you should be eating for a healthy and full life, I want to highlight a few things you need to be aware of.

When you stop drinking, or you're in the process of changing any other deep seated habit, there will always be the temptation to find impulsive relief using food, otherwise known as emotional eating. When you feel stressed, it can be very easy to dive into a tub of ice cream or a bar of chocolate. The problem with scratching this type of emotional itch is it will only give you pleasure momentarily and will fail utterly in dealing with your long-term emotions or the underlying stress that has stirred up these emotions. Even though the one bar of chocolate does you very little harm in the grand scheme of things, trying to solve your problems through eating is just another flawed coping mechanism that will lead to more problems than it solves.

Let's take a look at the how food interacts with your body and your life.

First I want to talk about what I call the three timelines of eating:

1. The immediate process of eating.

2. The short-term effects of that food on your body and mind.

3. The long-term effects of that food on your body and mind.

The first timeline is where you are in the process of eating. You handle the food, smell it, serve it, and eat it. The instant gratification temptation is relieved in this moment. You taste the food, enjoy the taste, and finally swallow and move on to the next mouth-full.

The second timeline is the duration that the food will spend inside your body. After you swallow each mouthful, you generally forget about it, it becomes part of your past. Unless you experience some problems with digestion or feeling full, you won't ever think about think about the food again. But the food is still there, the eating was only the beginning of its journey and interaction with you and your body. The food travels through your body, slowly being digested, and your body extracts what it can in terms of nutrients. What's left over is either stored as fat or eliminated as waste. The timeline of this process varies widely with each individual. It can take anywhere from a few hours to a few days.

The third timeline is what happens to your body in the long-term as a consequence of your food choices today including weight gain or disease. How do your food choices affect your internal organs over a period of a decade or two? Does the food contribute to plaque build-up along the walls of your arteries? How does it affect your life expectancy?

For the purposes of this book, I'm going to concentrate on the second timeline. As the food interacts with your body, moving through your digestive tract and breaking down, you get lots of feedback. You need to be conscious of this feedback, of how the food is making you feel, and how it influences and alters your present state of mind. Up until now, you've enjoyed the instant gratification of the first timeline, the comfort eating phase. But now that the food is inside you, becoming a part of you, how do you feel? Do you feel relaxed? Do you feel stressed? Do you feel that you're fueled for dealing with the stress of your habit change? Do you feel your willpower increase or decrease? Or have you just added to the pressure your body is already experiencing?

Hang Loose Without Booze is about making better and healthier choices that benefit your emotions and bolster your determination to succeed with the changes want to make in your life. Emotional eating might give you the instant gratification hit in the moment, but the relief you feel never lasts. The effect of your food choices on your body are long-lasting.

As I said, the purpose of this entire section is to get you to think about what you're putting into your mouth, the good and the bad. I'm not suggesting that you shouldn't eat so-called 'bad' foods at all, although I would still advise caution. You can enjoy yourself with food as a natural part of a normal and healthy life. To deny yourself the pleasures which only your taste buds can deliver will do more harm than good in the long run. However, you need to avoid eating to satisfy your impulsive emotional triggers. You can't eat your way out of stress, worry, anger, loneliness, and so on. The last thing you want to do is replace one false friend with another.

What to Do

1. Look for the things, people, places, and thoughts that are triggering your emotional eating.

2. Use this book, and its companion *Hang Loose Without Booze* 2, to look for other emotionally satisfying and less destructive methods of controlling your feelings.

3. When you feel a craving to emotionally eat, hit your pause button for a moment and think about what you're doing.

4. In the long-term, you need to build a healthy lifestyle with plenty of exercise and good nutrition.

3. Eat More Frequently with Smaller Portions

One of the biggest obstacles to you feeling relaxed and happy is when you don't have enough physical energy. Eating the traditional three square meals can overload your digestive system 3 times a day and cause you to feel bloated. This overload plays havoc with your energy levels. To avoid this, eat more frequently and in smaller portions. You will still be eating the same amount of food, but you're stretching it over six or seven meals instead of the usual three. This is known as grazing.

Grazing makes much more sense in terms of human evolution. When our ancestors lived in the wild, there were times of plenty and other times of famine. In general, our ancestors got their food where they could find it, often needing to travel long distances to gather and scavenge. This meant eating on the go and often.

Harley Street doctor, Antony Haynes says "Grazing was the way our body was designed to eat. Large meals burden the digestive system, often causing bloating and lowered energy while the body struggles to digest them. By eating smaller meals you prevent this, and the body functions more efficiently throughout the day."

This regular intake of food is much more likely to maintain your blood sugar levels, stabilize your energy levels, and make life easier to cope with.

What to Do

1. Because you are probably already eating in the traditional 3-meals-a-day fashion, with snacks in between, you don't really need to change that much except the portion size of your main meals. Split these meals into six instead of 3.

2. Each meal doesn't have to be the same size, but try not to overload your system with too much food at any one sitting.

3. You can make sure you're eating smaller portions by using smaller plates when you dish up your food.

4. Don't put the pots or serving dishes on the table where it's easy to dip in for seconds. If you want more food you'll have to get up from the table and walk to the pot for a second helping.

5. Learn to eat until satisfied instead of eating to be full.

4. Skip Ropes, Not Breakfast

We've all heard versions of the saying, 'you should always get a good breakfast inside you before you start the day' or 'breakfast is the most important meal of the day'. Why is that? Here are 5 reasons:

1. People who skip breakfast are more likely to gain weight. One theory is that by skipping breakfast, people are likely to eat more at lunchtime and with snacks during the day. You're playing catchup for the rest of the day.

2. Good quality early nutrition fires you up. When you eat a carbohydrate intense food for breakfast, such as whole wheat bread or cereal, you boost your energy levels for the day.

3. Start as you mean to go on. There's an old saying which says, life is too short to start your day with broken pieces of yesterday. You should always eat a good breakfast as part of a morning routine. As we've seen, eating a healthy breakfast puts your body into a good place for the day. Your mind also feels the benefits of this early fueling, which I'll talk about more in the next section. Putting this all together and you have a recipe for a good day. An early morning routine sets the tone for rest of the day, it puts you on the right track. I begin my morning routine with a half-liter of water, followed by 4 or 5 bananas. Then I go for a walk or take some other form of exercise, and finally I either sit for some meditation for half an hour or catch up on some reading. If I miss out on this routine for some reason, I always feel the worse for wear and never get as much done.

4. An all-round breakfast bucks your mood. I remember a

piece of advice I got from one of my first employer. My job was fixing lawn mowers in a factory near where I lived in Dublin during my school summer holidays. My boss was a complete asshole, but his father was such a kindly old gent who was always willing to share his wisdom. Besides telling me not to take any notice of his grumpy son, he'd always ask if I had eaten my breakfast. He told me, "An empty sack always falls". Good sage advice. Your brain runs on the food you eat. That first meal sets your mood for the day. Eat wisely.

5. Breakfast can boost your willpower. Some people call it willpower and others call it self-control, either way it's an essential part of the process of change. Exercising your willpower is like using a muscle, the more you use is during the day, the more tired it becomes. But constant use also makes it stronger in the long-term. Let me explain. Willpower fuel comes in two parts - practice and energy. Practice builds strong willpower and the right fuel helps maintain willpower stamina. Building your willpower muscles takes consistent practice over time, so you can't rely on that in the beginning. However, if you feed your body the right fuel every day you provide the immediate energy you need for strong self-control. The right fuel begins with a good breakfast.

What to Do

1. After your morning ablutions, eat your breakfast.

2. Make a good breakfast a part of a regular morning routine

3. Don't wait any more than half an hour to eat your meal.

4. Choose something healthy, high in complex carbs and protein, and avoid foods which are high in sugar, fat, or salt.

5. Eating With Intention While Paying Attention

What is Mindfulness and Why Should You Be Mindful When You Eat?

Mindfulness is the act of being in the moment and concentrating fully on what you are doing. Mindfulness in eating means taking the time to appreciate the food in front of you and the whole process of dining.

Mindful eating is about being enthusiastic and paying attention to how your food looks, seeing the different colors and textures, being careful and attentive in preparing the ingredients, absorbing the rich aromas of the cooking and the finished dishes, the textures as you put the food in your mouth, and finally enjoying the taste.

There are plenty of reasons to be mindful when you eat, here are just three:

1. Eating is one of the most basic needs in our life. We need food to survive. But sitting down to a meal means much more than that. There is a simple pleasure to be found in eating that goes way beyond just satisfying your hunger. The act of eating brings out something elemental in all of us, almost primeval. Think about what food really means to us. If we were living in the wild, it would mean we were going to survive for another day. Finding the food to feed yourself and your family would be a full time job. When you put that food into your mouth, it signifies the end of the hunt, the satisfaction in knowing that you did well that day.

2. Focusing on the food and not on the TV builds your self-control muscles. Eating mindfully is a form of meditation, a break in the day, a respite from pressure, and a chance to re-energize. When you eat mindfully, you extract the energy from the nutrients in the food, you also re-energize through the mindfulness process.

3. Mindfulness helps you better enjoy your food. How many times have you sat down to a meal in front of the television, or while reading a newspaper, and by the time the meal is over, you can't remember a single mouthful. You didn't notice anything about the food, not even the taste. By being mindful, you slow yourself down, you stay in the moment, and you enjoy eating your food. These are some of the small pleasures that we seem to have forgotten in our mad rush through life. But it's these small pleasures that add depth and volume to your bank of accumulated enjoyment. More enjoyment leads to more happiness. More happiness leads to feeling less stressed and more relaxed. When you have a full bank of accumulated enjoyment at your disposal, who needs to get wasted?

What to Do

Make a meal out of it. Eating mindfully is very simple, you don't have to overelaborate.

1. Cut the distractions. Try to eliminate as many distractions as you can. This means turning off the television, the radio, putting away your books and newspapers, leave your phone somewhere else. Focus your attention on the eating and the dining experience, staying in the moment.

2. Focus on what you are about to eat. Take the time to be grateful for the food in front of you. Use all your senses to appreciate each dimension of the food as you slowly make your way through your meal. Think of it like a mini-journey.

3. Think about a train and chew-chew. One way of slowing down your eating is to chew each mouthful as if you are tasting it for the first time. A good chew-chew target is to chomp your food about 20 times before swallowing. You'll enjoy the food much more and give your digestive system less work to do. This is an

area that I've really had to work at in my own life. I used to gallop my way through my food like someone was just about to snatch the plate from under my nose. I don't know if it was because I was raised in a big working class family with little money. There's nine of us, but I was one of the biggest, so I don't think it's that. More likely I ate fast so I could get second helpings before anyone else got to the pot. I was a growing lad after all!

6. Meals and Memories are Made Here - Sitting to Eat

When I think about my grandmother, I remember that she had this wonderful old-fashioned kitchen with a massive wooden dining table, all scarred up with age and the stains from the thousands of meals that she'd served on it over the years. Every time we visited her home, we'd be ushered to that table and we knew we were in for a treat. It could be a slice of cake and a cup of milky tea, some toast and jam, or if we were lucky one of her delicious home-cooked dinners.

I remember that when you went into her house through the front door, you walked into a carpeted hallway with old photos in picture frames along the wall to the left and a wooden staircase leading upstairs to the right. The carpet had a word patch right down the middle which led straight into that old kitchen. Hanging on the kitchen door, just below the glass panel, was a blue and white porcelain sign, the kind you see in old Dutch kitchens, which simply said, "Meals and Memories are Made Here". The sign was right, I remember lots of meals and plenty of great memories in that kitchen, of those meals, and my smiling Gran with her frilly aprons. Those days seem so long ago now, but I still remember them very clearly.

We all live busy lives and it can sometimes seem difficult to take the time for enjoying our food. We're so occupied with pursuing the things which seem 'more important' that we give a very low priority to one of the most important aspects of our lives, eating. We don't prepare enough of our food, nor do we take the time in eating it, often hurrying it down as quickly as possible, before moving on to the next thing.

Sitting while you eat, even if it's just for a snack, is an essential building block for establishing that mindful eating ritual that I spoke about in the previous section. Did you know that your digestive system functions much more efficiently when you're relaxed and stress-free? Sitting to eat your food helps you to relax, to focus on the food, thereby aiding your digestive processes.

If you're not used to sitting and being mindful in your eating, preferring instead to multi-task at mealtimes, it can be difficult for you in the beginning. So just sitting at a table to eat can be a very useful first step. Relaxation will come with practice. Eventually your body will get into the habit of automatically chilling-out whenever you sit to eat. Once you've become accustomed to being seated for all your meals, then you can start implement some of the other aspects of mindful eating.

What to Do

1. Have one place in your home which is purely reserved for eating, preferably at a table with upright chairs. If you're stuck for space in your home, you can always buy a foldaway table and chairs.

2. Sitting to eat with other people will make for some of your fondest memories.

7. Don't Stress About Eating Perfectly

We live in a world which is swamped with information about food, nutrition, and dieting. But what exactly makes a perfect meal? It's hard to know. I still struggle with some of the most basic of food related questions. I bet you're the same. Are you worried about eating a balanced diet? Are you eating too much fat, sugar, or salt? Do you think should be eating more of one particular type of food or avoiding another altogether? As you sit down to your meal, do you think about what the food is going do to you in the long-term?

Thinking too much about your diet, what you should or shouldn't be eating and drinking, can lead to worry and stress. When you're under stress, making the right decisions about what you eat becomes even more challenging.

So what's the solution?

The best answer is that there's no such thing as *the* perfect diet. There are many factors that will lead you to making effective choices and most of these things are dependent on who YOU are.

What to Do

1. Focus on balance. When choosing what to eat and putting together your meal, try to find a balance between the three major food groups: carbohydrates, protein, and fat... yes - I did say fat. Fat is an essential part of your diet, you just need to eat the right types of fat. Good fat lowers your cholesterol, and helps you to control your moods, fatigue, weight, and maintain a highly active mind. The good fats are monounsaturated and polyunsaturated and can be found in vegetables and vegetable oils, nuts, beans, and

fatty fish like mackerel and salmon.

What does a balanced plate of food look like? Think about your plate with a cross drawn over it, dividing the plate into four equal sections. You should fill two of those quarters with vegetables, one quarter with a protein based food, and the other with a starch. For meat eaters, your protein can come from lean cuts of meat, turkey, chicken, or fish. The starch can come from potatoes, rice, beans, or lentils. I eat a plant-based diet, so I get my all my carbs, proteins, and fats from veg, grains, beans, and nuts.

2. Indulgence is good for you in small doses. A little indulgence is good for you, mentally and physically. It's a healthy part of a balanced diet and it's nothing to feel guilty about. When you do indulge, stick to a 50/50 approach. If you want to have your steak and chips, have a smaller portion - a few ounces of steak and half a portion of fries. Then balance the other half with some steamed veg or a healthy salad. Or have a healthy main course, sharing an indulgent dessert with your meal partner.

3. Enjoy the treat. Set aside a time, once a week perhaps, to enjoy a piece of cake or a bar of chocolate, if that's your thing. If you like potato chips, there's a time and a place as well. People get into trouble with these foods when they overindulge, when these 'treat foods' becomes a part of their normal diet.

4. Try not to eat for emotional comfort. If you absolutely must have a treat to satisfy a craving, have a small amount and be mindful when you eat it. Take the time to enjoy it.

8. Listen to What Your Body is Telling You

Being food mindful is about being in the moment, relaxing and enjoying your meals. It's also about understanding how your body and mind are reacting to the food you've just eaten.

When you used to drink, the alcohol put a lot of pressure on your digestive system. The constant input of toxins causes your defensive system to stay on full alert. Your body has to devote a large proportion of its energies into eliminating this threat. Now that you have removed alcohol from your body, your system will return to its natural state of activity. This means your digestive system can cope much better with many of the foods you eat. Finally your digestive system can concentrate on what it was designed to do: processing the food you put in, distributing the nutrients to where they are needed, and giving you the energy you need for life.

What to Do

1. Over time, and with the right diet, you'll become much more attuned to how your digestive system should feel. This is a skill that's going to take you a while to master. First you've got to understand what counts as normal for you. What was normal while you are drinking is no longer normal. To build this skill, you need to tune into the language of your body and pay attention to what it's trying to tell you. One of the best ways of doing this is to keep a food diary.

2. Start your food diary by taking notes about what you eat. Include each food, the time of day, how long each meal takes, and

how slow or fast you're eating. Ask yourself some questions. How you feel while you are eating? What about after the food has been in your belly for a few minutes, and again after an hour or two? Do you feel good? Do you feel satisfied? Are you feeling bloated or in pain? Do you feel tired? Do you feel energetic?

3. Over time, you will start to notice patterns between what you eat and how you feel and think. These patterns will be your guide as to which foods are causing a stressed reaction in your digestive system and which are not. It's only once you uncover these patterns that you'll be able to understand where any problems lie. Only then can you take some action. You can avoid the food altogether. You can also try to reduce the frequency of eating that particular food, maybe only eating it once or twice a week, instead of every day. You can also consume it in smaller amounts to see if that makes a difference.

4. If you are quitting alcohol, some of the foods you eat during the first few weeks of your quit might not agree with you once you stop drinking. This is because there will be a lot internal repair and rejuvenation work happening in your body. Don't forget that in these early days you still have the body of a drinker. Your organs don't know that the flood of alcohol is not going to come back. If one type of food causes you problems, avoid it for a while. Allow your body the time to go through the initial post-alcohol recovery phase. After a month or so, you can re-introduce the food into your diet in smaller portions and use your food diary to test the results.

9. Keeping Some Emergency Foods Handy

We all have those days when we just don't feel like cooking. Maybe you've had a hard day with the kids or at work, you've just received a hefty bill in the post, or you've had some bad news that you'd rather forget. The end result is the same - you can't be bothered with all that preparing and cooking. You don't want to even look at the kitchen, never mind use it. These are danger times for maintaining your nutrition. Shopping at these times can be like negotiating your way through an emotional minefield where it can be all too easy to fill your basket with all those tempting comfort foods that crowd for your attention across the shelves. They hold the promise of instant gratification, take minutes to heat or can be eaten straight from the packet.

To get through these stressed-out moments, while still maintaining good nutrition, it's a good idea to have some healthy emergency meals on hand.

What to Do

1. When you are preparing a meal under normal, non-stressed conditions, cook a little extra and set aside a portion or two for freezing. Then, when you're feeling a bit lazy or tired, you have some convenient meals waiting. All you have to do is warm in the microwave and eat. No hassle!

2. Have your breakfast for dinner. Breakfast is not the only time you can eat scrambled eggs on toast. Breakfast meals tend to be some of the easiest to prepare. Who needs complication first thing in the morning, right! Sometimes if I'm feeling tired, I'll make

a large bowl of porridge, honey, and bananas. It's dead simple to throw together, it fills me up, and I'm still getting a bucket load of nutrition. This is my default healthy comfort food.

3. Make a slow cooker meal. Slow cooking is one of the easiest methods of cooking, particularly if you just use the ingredients that you have on hand. You can prepare your meal the night before, turn on your slow cooker the next morning before you start your day, and you'll have a perfectly cooked healthy meal waiting for you in the evening. All that's left for you to do is to serve and enjoy.

4. Sometimes, it's the idea of prepping all the ingredients for the meal that puts you off. If you're tired, take a seat while you prep. Bring a tall stool to your counter while you chop your ingredients. Alternatively, take the ingredients to your dining table and prep them there.

5. Skip the cooking and take out. Another great way of beating your lack of enthusiasm for the kitchen is to pick up your phone and order a take-away. Take-out food should be the exception, rather than the rule. But there's no real reason not to indulge yourself every so often. To get the best of nutrition from your take-out meal, order only what looks like it's real food. Avoid burgers, chicken nuggets, and all that other processed junk. If you can't name the meat, presume the worse and don't buy, choose something else. Remember that fast food generally contains high percentages of sugar, salt, and the wrong types of fat. You are paying for the food so don't be afraid to ask for it to be cooked to your liking.

6. Mix the good with the not so good. You can cut the salt, sugar, or fat content of any product by dilution. For instance, reduce the overall salt in a tin of soup by throwing a cup or two of frozen veggies into the same pot. This will dilute the salt percentage in each serving. For an instant salad that's not too heavy on the fat, take a tub of coleslaw and mix it with a large bowl of fresh salad ingredients.

Foods to Avoid - Introduction

Nutritionist and whole foods advocate, Ann Wigmore, once said "The food you eat can be either the safest and most powerful form of medicine or the slowest form of poison." Real health care comes in the form of exercise and nutrition, not in a packet of pills. Pills only care for the already sick.

When you quit drinking, you're making a real transformation. It's not just about stopping the alcohol flow, you have to change many elements your life, and your nutrition should be right up there at the top of that list. If you only remove the alcohol, but carry on eating a bad diet, don't expect to get much different results.

In a later section, we're going to take a more in-depth look at the kinds of food which will reduce your stress and help you maintain better levels of relaxation, but this is only one part of the equation. The other part is avoiding the foods which offer you no physical benefit and will only increase your stress levels.

As we've seen previously, most indulgent foods are fine when eaten in very moderate amounts, but even then you should try to substitute a healthier version whenever you can. These healthier versions are available, you just have to look a bit harder.

There are also some easy ingredient substitutions that will help you to create much healthier versions of almost any type of dish.

In the next few sections, I'm going to go over some of the more common foods you should avoid and why.

10. Simple or Complex Carbs - What's the Deal?

Just as all calories are not made equal, not every carb is good for you. On the flip side, carbohydrates have gained such a bad reputation in the diet world. Crazy diets, such as the Atkins diet, fool people into believing that the reason they are putting on weight is because they are eating all those carbohydrates - such bullshit! What matters in terms of carbohydrates is the quality and type of carb that you eat, and of course which carbs you avoid.

Your ability to walk, run, swim, work, rest, play, or just breathe hinges on the ability of your body to extract the energy it needs from the food you eat. The primary fuel of choice for your body is glucose. Carbohydrates are the most readily broken down source of glucose. So you do your body a big disservice by not giving it what it wants.

Not eating carbohydrates is also bad for your stress levels. If you want to stay strong, get to and remain at your peak mental and physical performance, you need to eat your carbs.

In a later section, we'll take a look at some good carbs that you should be regularly eating, fruits and vegetable, nuts, beans, lentils, and so on. For now, we're going to stick to the carbs you should avoid?

Sugar is one form of simple carbohydrate that you should avoid, as you will see in the next section, but there are many others. Simple carbs put your body through a roller coaster effect of highs and lows. Your feelings are affected, as are your energy levels, along with your moods. When your body digests simple carbs, they are broken down and absorbed into the system very quickly. That initial rush you feel when you eat a food containing these simple carbs is always followed by a later dip. It's this plunge down the carbohydrate roller coaster that causes you to feel lethargic and depressed.

The simple carbs found in highly processed foods don't come with enough natural fiber. It's this natural fiber that allows the sugars to be released more steadily. Many processed simple carbs, such as white bread, white pasta, and cakes, are lacking in the essential nutrients that help maintain your health and stability. These empty calories contribute to weight gain and obesity, run your system down instead of picking it up, and can lead to mental suffering.

What to Do

1. For those who are quitting alcohol, you need to give your body the fuel it needs to do the job of returning your body to full toxic-free health. Don't get too caught up in the instant gratification eating that simple processed carbs offer. This type of eating may satisfy your taste buds, but once these foods are in your body they don't provide any value. In fact, this type of rubbish food will often retard the post-alcohol clean-up processes.

2. Replace processed foods with whole foods as often as you can. We'll look at this more in a later section.

11. Hiding the Poison with Sugar'd Words

The number one food to avoid, if you want to boost your chances of having a stress-free life, is processed-sugar. Here are a few reasons:

1. Sugar can overload an already overloaded liver.

A diet containing lots of processed sugars can lead to fatty liver syndrome. On its own, this condition does not represent an immediate health concern. Over time though, the fat can build up, which can lead to liver swelling, and eventual liver cirrhosis. When you quit drinking alcohol, your liver has spent a few years already being overloaded. Now it's a good idea to help your liver, giving it a chance to recover. The last thing you want to do is put more pressure onto this already tortured and crucial organ.

2. Desserts equals Stressed

In his book, The Bitter Truth About Sugar, Dr Robert Lustig says "It's no coincidence that desserts spelled backwards is stressed. Cortisol (a hormone we release in response to stress) specifically increases our desire for comfort foods. Over several years, prolonged cortisol release leads to excessive intake of high-fat and high-sugar foods."

3. Sugar is Not the Only Problem

Sweet foods not only contain massive quantities of sugar, these products are also packed with other dubious ingredients. Apart from the fat content of most pastries and cakes, which we'll take a look at in the next section, most processed sweet foods are filled with preservatives, colorings, and other nasty additives that are not good for your health or your stress levels.

What to do

First, avoid processed sugar in all its many forms.

Here's a few foods to eat which will satisfy your cravings, are packed with nutrients that your body needs, and can help your body to recover a healthy balance.

1. **Nuts**. Nuts contain large amounts of essential nutrients which will actively help lower your stress and heal your immune system.

2. **Berries**. When berries are in season they can provide you with all the sweetness you need along with a blast from all that vitamin C and other micronutrients. When not in season, you can use frozen or tinned berries. Buy the tinned berries which are canned in their own natural juice, not in sugary syrup.

3. **Dried Fruits**. Dried fruits are also a good substitute during the off-season. They still contain the same amount of natural sugar as their fresh counterparts. Be careful of the calories though. Pound for pound, the fresh version contains fewer calories. Dried fruits have been dehydrated, reducing their weight and increasing their overall calorie count.

12. Crisps, Pretzels, and the Trans Fat De-Railway

Trans fats give processed foods taste and texture, while extending their shelf life. Unfortunately, the price for this indulgence is often paid with your health. Trans fat laden foods are disappearing from our supermarket shelves, but this not the only type of fat you should avoid if you want to relax and reduce your levels of stress. All high fat foods, especially foods which are high in saturated fats, can be detrimental. High fat foods thicken your blood and make you feel lethargic.

What to Do

Here's some foods to avoid:

1. Anything deep fat fried or battered.

2. Anything labeled as containing trans fats.

3. Most store bought ice creams.

4. Crisp/Pretzels/Crackers

5. Frozen dinners.

6. French fries

7. Pancakes and waffles

8. Fried Chicken

9. Non-dairy creamers

10. Microwave popcorn

11. Ground beef

12. Cookies

13. Meat sticks

14. Canned Chili

15. Packaged puddings

If you would like to know more about the food you are eating, particularly the processed foods, read the book *Salt Sugar Fat: How the Food Giants Hooked Us* by Michael Moss. It offers an alarming insight into how the food industry attempts to addict us to consuming and over-eating their products.

The author says, "Inevitably, the manufacturers of processed food argue that they have allowed us to become the people we want to be, fast and busy, no longer slaves to the stove. But in their hands, the salt, sugar, and fat they have used to propel this social transformation are not nutrients as much as weapons—weapons they deploy, certainly, to defeat their competitors but also to keep us coming back for more."

And about the manufacturers themselves, he has this to say, "As a culture, we've become upset by the tobacco companies advertising to children, but we sit idly by while the food companies do the very same thing. And we could make a claim that the toll taken on the public health by a poor diet rivals that taken by tobacco."

13. Beware the 'Health Food' Labels!

Here's some good advice from American author Micheal Pollan about where to find the best sources of nutrition and health in the foods you eat. He says, "If it came from a plant, eat it. If it was made in a plant, don't." Most of our food industry pays no attention to the health of its customers. And unfortunately, we are treated by a health care industry that pays no attention to the food that we eat. We spend way too much time in counting calories when we should really be concentrating our math skills on counting chemicals.

There's an old saying that goes, "Beware of the half-truth. You may have gotten hold of the wrong half."

Foods that are labeled as 'healthy' often contain unhealthy ingredients, making them not as healthy as you would like to believe, or that the food industry would have us believe.

The food industry is very enterprising, I'll give it that. Processed food manufacturers understand that we all want to live healthy lives. Part of that deep seated need of ours is to eat healthy foods, but we are driven by taste as much as by nutrition.

These companies also know that we lead very busy lives, so we can be manipulated into opting for convenience over spending hours in the kitchen, slaving over a hot stove.

A third piece of their psychological armory is that we always look for information that reinforces what we already believe, or that supports what we want to believe. This is known as the confirmation bias. If you like eating pizza and you spot a magazine article that tells you about the health benefits of eating a four cheese super slice, you aren't likely to pursue the evidence further.

Given that we want to eat healthy, we want convenience, and we'll readily accept our nutritional information at face value, the food industry has invented a whole list of *magic* words that they print on their packaging to portray health and convenience. Words like 'fat free', 'whole grain', 'gluten-free', 'natural', 'farm-fed', 'sugar-free', 'fresh', 'healthy', 'organic', or 'naturally sweetened', to name but a few.

Here's an example. Would you buy a product that said it contained 'Evaporated Cane Juice'? In my mind, that sounds healthy. Florida Crystals is one of the companies that manufacture this product. On its website*, Florida Crystals describes the process of making their product as one which preserves "the original sun-sweetened flavor, and product-enhancing attributes. Our product line consists of organic and natural offerings that contain no artificial additives or preservatives." That would have me sold. I'd even pay more for the benefits of getting a sun-sweetened flavor!

Judy Sanchez, a spokesperson for the United States Sugar Corporation**, another Florida based sugar business, puts things into perspective by saying, "All sugar is evaporated cane juice, they [Florida Crystals] just use that for a natural-sounding name for a product." The only real difference between evaporated cane juice and ordinary white sugar is the evaporated cane juice has traces of molasses. But, it's ultimately the same thing, processed sugar. It has no health benefits at all. It's no better or worse.

What to Do

How do you get past all the slime and double-talk?

1. Make sure you carefully read all the nutritional labels. Take your glasses to the store and see what's in the product you're thinking of eating. I'm not kidding about your glasses. You might have to buy a pair of spectacles just to read some of these nutritional labels, the writing is so small.

2. The ingredients are listed according to their quantity. The first ingredient on the list is the largest ingredient by volume and

so on.

3. The only way to guarantee you're getting healthy foods is to avoid foods that come with labels and buy whole foods from a well-known and trusted source. The food we can grow on this planet, naturally provides us with everything we need to survive. The word manufacture, when mentioned in the same sentence as food, should make you wary, if not scary, about what it is you are putting into your body.

What has this to do with relaxing? Most of these sneaky ingredients are the enemy of relaxation and are best friends with stress.

*https://www.floridacrystals.com/content/192/evaporated-cane-juice-products.aspx

**http://www.npr.org/sections/thesalt/2012/10/18/163098211/evaporated-cane-juice-sugar-in-disguise

14. Stop Eating Products that Just Look Like Food but are Not!

I'm going to keep this one short. You don't really need me to tell you the dangers of eating fast foods or the damage that the fast food industry has done to our society. A study, conducted by the University of Navarra, Spain in 2009, looked at how people were affected after they switched from the traditional Spanish diet, or the Mediterranean diet, to a fast food type diet.

The study was set up to ascertain if there were obvious physical signs of ill health, such as diabetes and heart disease, as a result of the switch. They also measured the overall change in mental health.

What they found from studying these 10,000 patients was that those who remained on the traditional Mediterranean diet were half as likely to develop symptoms of depression as those who ate a diet full of unhealthy processed and junk food.* Two further studies, one in the UK** and one in Australia*** confirmed these results.

What to Do

I'll keep this simple and short.

1. Avoid processed or fast food.

2. Eat whole foods from trusted sources.

* http://www.ncbi.nlm.nih.gov/pubmed/19805699

** http://www.ncbi.nlm.nih.gov/pubmed/19880930

***http://www.ncbi.nlm.nih.gov/pubmed/20048020

15. Food Stress-Busters

Eating plays a large part in helping you to feel your best. It's the primary way of fueling your body and mind, but too often we treat food as just another form of entertainment. First we consider how good the food tastes, *then* we think about the nutritional value. In reality, it should be the other way around. We should look for foods that are good for you first, then look for healthy ways of making that food more interesting or more entertaining.

Eating for entertainment, or comfort, generally leads to some questionable food choices. Our bodies instinctively crave fat, sugar, and salt, and there's nothing wrong with that. We need fat, sugar, and salt for a variety of reasons. We have evolved to thrive and survive in the natural world where these things are in short supply. But they have become more than readily available in large quantities through your local supermarket and fast food chains. We all know the results. At one time, only kings and the very wealthy were fat or obese. Now, so many people are obese, it's being called an epidemic.

In terms of looking and feeling your best, getting the most out of your life, and avoiding some of the most common forms of mental and physical illness, good nutrition should be on the top of your list. Hippocrates, one of the most important figures in the history of medicine, said, "Let food be thy medicine and medicine be thy food".

In his book, *Whole: Rethinking the Science of Nutrition*, T. Colin Campbell writes along similar lines. He says, "The foods you consume can heal you faster and more profoundly than the most expensive prescription drugs, and more dramatically than the most extreme surgical interventions, with only positive side effects".

What to Do

1. As we've seen earlier, there's absolutely nothing wrong with indulging yourself so long as you exercise caution and restraint. If you don't, you'll likely face much greater challenges in your future, challenges you might not be able to overcome. If you are going to indulge, exchange the unhealthy for the healthy wherever you can and choose a smaller portion size.

I love eating sweets and biscuits. If I open a packet of biscuits while I'm watching some evening TV, I can go through the entire packet without even thinking about it. To avoid this, I separate the full packet into single serving sized portions. Then I put them into plastic boxes or jiffy bags. When I feel like a snack, it's easy to just grab a single portion.

2. Reduce the amount of snacking you do by eating more regularly and slower. Break your meals up into 5 or 6 sittings instead of the traditional three and be mindful with every mouthful.

3. Choose whole foods wherever you can.

The foods we'll look at over the coming pages are nutritious and healthy. What's more, they'll help you to relax and feel less stressed. Again, some restraint is still required, even with some of the healthier alternatives, such as the nuts and dark chocolate. Just because these foods are good for you, don't go overboard.

16. No Such Thing as a Little Garlic

Garlic is a great all-rounder for your body. If you have just quit drinking alcohol, garlic can be classed as one of the superfoods that can help repair some of the damage that you've done to your liver and other internal organs.

Garlic will also help your body to detox. Garlic has been used for thousands of years as a potent medicine. The antiviral and antibacterial qualities help you to maintain a healthy immune system and regulate your blood sugar levels.

To get the best out of garlic, or any other superfood, you should eat it in its whole or nearest to whole state.

In his book, *The Healing Benefits of Garlic*, Dr John Heinerman writes about a survey of 8500 people who had reached their 100th birthday. The two things that stood out most in their diets was the consumption of garlic and onions.

What to Do

1. If you can, eat the garlic raw.

2. Try to buy the freshest garlic, which is also the mildest.

3. Rinse the crushed garlic under a running tap. This will remove some of the sulfur compounds that cause the harsh aroma.

4. Add garlic to hummus, guacamole, or mix it with some cottage cheese, then spread the mixture onto a piece of whole-wheat toast.

5. When you slice garlic, you not only release that pungent garlic smell, you also release the health-giving properties such as allicin. To get the most out of these healthy properties, let the

garlic sit for at least five minutes after you've chopped it, preferably ten, which allows the allicin to form. This is especially important if you are going to cook the garlic. To maintain the maximum nutrients in the garlic, don't cook for more than 15 minutes.

6. If you're worried about garlic breath, you can chew on a piece of parsley or a coffee bean, suck on a lemon wedge or drink some green tea. You can also mask the smell with some sugar-free chewing gum.

17. I Love You, Honey

Honey is another food that's been used for its healing properties throughout the world over thousands of years. The ancient Egyptians used it as a form of currency and the American Indians used it as a basis for much of their herbal medicines.

In his book, *The Happiness Diet: A Nutritional Prescription for a Sharp Brain, Balanced Mood, and Lean, Energized Body*, Dr. Drew Ramsey says "Honey helps reduce inflammation, which is very important to maintaining a healthy brain. Some depression actually stems from chronic, low-grade inflammation."

What to Do

1. Use honey in place of sugar in your cooking. This natural sweetener can be used in all kinds of home-made cakes and desserts. It can also be added to sauces and dressings, giving them a rich golden color and taste.

2. Honey infused herbs. Honey added to herbal tea makes a delicious pick-me-up. To get the most out of your honey and herb infusions, let the herbs steep in the honey for a couple of weeks before using. You can also use the mix as a quick energizer. Simply add a teaspoon of honey to your favorite herbal tea.

If you do decide to try the two-week infusion, some of the best herbs to use are lemon balm, valerian, passionflower, catnip, or skullcap.

You can use a single herb or a combination.

Vary the quantities of herbs depending on how strong you want the infusion. More herbs equals a stronger tasting infusion.

Use enough honey to cover the herbs. Simply mix the ingredients in a sterilized jar and let the concoction steep for a couple of weeks. When done, you can use the infusion in teas, spread on toast, or in a salad dressing; just use your imagination. There's more on stress-buster drinks in the next section.

3. Take a bath of milk and honey

As you run your bath, pour one or two cups of milk (cows, almond, soy, or any other milk) and a half cup of honey under the flowing tap. Swish your hand around in the water until all the ingredients are dissolved. Then lay down in the water, relax, close your eyes, and let your thoughts drift.

I don't use honey anymore since I started eating a plant based diet. When I used to eat it, my favorite was a simple spread of honey over a piece of toast. Eating a piece of toast, covered in honey, before you go to bed can help you to sleep. Along with the calming properties of honey, the carbs in the toast give you a quick spike of energy followed by a crash of tiredness. Perfect for a midnight snack. Now I substitute maple syrup for honey which seems to have the same effect.

18. Has Everyone Gone Bananas?

Bananas are one of Mother Nature's most complete foods.

Bananas are a great source of magnesium and potassium which are known to be muscle relaxants. Bananas also help the brain to produce the relaxing neurotransmitters serotonin and melatonin, by converting a protein in the bananas called tryptophan. The only way your body gets tryptophan is through your diet. Other important health benefits you'll get from eating bananas include lower blood pressure and cancer risk, better digestion and memory.

What to Do

1. Just peel and eat a banana or three.

2. Add a banana to some juice and blend.

3. Make banana ice-cream.

Bananas are one of my favorite foods. I eat at least 5 every day, sometimes as many as ten. They are my default fast food on the go. Generally, I just eat them straight out of the peel or in a smoothie. Because I only eat plant based foods, I don't eat dairy products. This used to mean that I missed out on ice-cream, which I love. That was until someone showed me how to make a delicious home-made banana ice-cream, which is unbelievably simple to make, much easier than making regular home-made ice-cream, that's for sure.

All you need is one ingredient, bananas, and you don't need to invest in an ice cream maker either. Take a few very ripe bananas. You know they are super ripe when they have black spots all over their skin. Peel the bananas and cut or break them into small pieces, about an inch long. Pop the banana pieces into a freezer bag and put them in the freezer overnight. Once fully frozen, place the sliced bananas into a food processor and turn on. You'll probably need to stop and redistribute the contents every few seconds until the processor blades can bite into the frozen chunks.

And that's it!

You'll end up with delicious tasting and very healthy ice cream.

19. Dark Chocolate is the Answer! What was the Question?

Dark chocolate is another great source of tryptophan, that essential amino acid that's responsible for serotonin production in your brain.

In her book, *Why Women Need Chocolate*, Deborah Waterhouse says that chocolate is "Mother Nature's solution via food cravings to try to elevate those chemicals, help us feel better and to function more efficiently". She goes on to say that you only need a small amount of chocolate to help bring your 'feel good' chemicals back into balance.

The reason dark chocolate is considered a better option than milk chocolate is because it contains more cacao beans than sugar. This helps provide the maximum health impact while avoiding the sugar crash.

What to Do

1. Use portion control. Remember that chocolate is high in calories. You won't stay relaxed in the long term if you're gaining weight from eating too much chocolate. It's all about balance.

2. Be mindful and take your time. Before you eat your piece of dark chocolate, take the time to have a good long sniff, savoring that special chocolaty aroma. Even the aroma of dark chocolate is enough to trigger a relaxation response in your brain. Once you pop a square in your mouth, don't chomp it down too quickly. Take your time to appreciate the taste and texture. Let the chocolate melt in your mouth. Swirl it around your tongue,

enjoying the aromas, flavors, and smoothness.

3. Use dark chocolate as a replacement for the other sweets in your diet. Because there's much less sugar in dark chocolate, by replacing the other sweets in your diet with dark chocolate you will be reducing the overall calories in your diet.

4. When you're shopping for your dark chocolate, look for a bar with at least 70% cocoa.

20. Love Nuts. Be Nuts

Nuts and seeds are another excellent source of tryptophan. They're also rich in some of the vitamins and minerals that help your brain relax including magnesium, zinc, and selenium. Selenium boosts your immune system, magnesium is also known as the energy mineral, and zinc is a necessary component in every protein your body makes.

There are many different ways to integrate nuts and seeds into your diet. They can also be stashed in your pocket or handbag for a quick snack when you're feeling peckish.

Writing for the New England Journal of Medicine, Dr. Frank Hu, Professor of Nutrition and Epidemiology at the Harvard School of Public Health, and Professor of Medicine at Harvard Medical School, says, "We found that people who ate nuts every day lived longer, healthier lives than people who didn't eat nuts". He adds, "Nuts are high in protein and fiber, which delays absorption and decreases hunger".

Which is the perfect nut? There's no such thing. Some nuts contain more of one nutrient than another and some have more fat than others. Your perfect nut depends on what you like to eat. Eat your favorite or choose a bag of mixed nuts.

What to Do

1. Choose unsalted instead of salted.

2. Try mixed nuts instead of sticking to one type.

3. Sprinkle some crushed nuts on your breakfast cereal or your morning yogurt.

4. Use crushed nuts in your salads or stir fries.

5. Spread peanut butter over some toast as a midnight snack to help you relax and sleep. Buy the healthiest brand you can find. Look for brands with low salt, oil, and sugar.

6. Use portion control. 100 calories of nuts is roughly equal to a small handful.

21. Celery Stick?

Celery is another amazing superfood which has a long history of medicinal use. Hippocrates would prescribe this plant to patients who were suffering from nervous tension. In 30 AD, the Roman encyclopaedist Aulius Cornelius Celsus, used celery seeds to relieve pain.

Today, nutritionists advise their patients to regularly eat celery for lowering blood pressure. Other reasons for eating celery include its cleansing and detoxing properties, treating kidney stones, and it can reduce inflammation in your body. It's also another natural sleep enhancer.

What to Do

1. If you like making homemade juice, add a stick of celery to the juicer for that extra bit of super goodness.

2. Add chopped celery to your stews. If, like me, you don't really enjoy the taste of celery, this is a great way getting it into your diet.

3. Add some celery leaves to your daily salad.

22. It's Not the Horse That Draws the Cart, but the Oats

Oatmeal is made from ground oats and is another natural whole food that's been used for a long time in treating stress and aiding relaxation. As well as lowering your stress levels, a bowl of porridge a day is known to reduce bad cholesterol, lower your risk of heart disease and type 2 diabetes, and can enhance your immune system. It can also be a great comfort food that won't make you fat, depending on what else you add to it, of course. Oats are rich in complex carbohydrates and fiber which helps to stabilize your blood sugar levels throughout the day, which is why it makes a great breakfast meal.

What to Do

1. Only use the old-fashioned type oats. Instant oats are processed and usually come packaged with lots of salt, sugar and other unhealthy ingredients. Make sure you read the labels.

2. Add a small handful of nuts or berries to your morning porridge for extra healthy brownie points.

3. If you like baking, use oatmeal as the base for your cookies instead of regular flour.

One of my favorite ways of using oatmeal is in combination with whizzed-up bananas. I blend two or three bananas with a third of a cup of water. Then I pour the mixture over a portion of raw oatmeal. Then I leave the mixture in the fridge overnight for a very healthy and delicious breakfast the next morning, full of healthy nutrition and brain food.

23. Magnesium - The Missing Link to Better Health

Magnesium is not a food, strictly speaking, but it's one of the most critical minerals for fighting off stress and helping you to relax. Magnesium is a mineral that plays a large part in maintaining a healthy heart and immune system. Magnesium can help to regulate your blood sugar levels, maintain strong teeth and healthy bones, and is an essential element in the natural detoxification process. Magnesium also helps produce the energy you need for your mental well-being, for strong self-belief and self-control.

What to Do

Here are some foods to eat which are high in magnesium:

1. Sunflower seeds. These are also high other nutrients for a healthy heart. Best eaten raw

2. Pumpkin seeds. Eating a handful of pumpkin seeds can account for 40% of your daily magnesium needs. They are also packed with protein, zinc, and manganese. Again, eat raw for the best results.

3. Any type of beans. To reduce the gas-production, soak them overnight.

4. Oats.

5. Dark Chocolate.

6. Almonds, cashews, Brazil nuts, pecans, walnuts, or just about any nut.

7. Avocado. If you simply add one slice of avocado to your salad or lunchtime sandwich, you will get 20 percent of all your magnesium needs.

8. Figs. One of my favorites. Try to buy them fresh. If you can't get them fresh, dried are a great substitute.

24. Fruit - The Healthy Fast Food

Fruit is just fantastic for your health and makes the perfect fast food. If you're feeling lethargic, eat a piece of fruit. If you need a quick pick-me-up in the middle of the day, eat some fruit. If you need an energy boost half-way through your workout routine, crack open a banana or crunch into the body of an apple. You don't need to add any seasonings to make fruit taste great, it's just perfect on its own. Fruit is low on the glycemic index. This is because it has a variety of sugars which are digested into your body at different rates. The fiber in fruit slows this process down even further. Fruit also contains a lot of water, making it a drink as well as a food.

One famous German study* put 120 subjects under stress by asking them to complete a math problem while public speaking. Half the test subjects were given a dose of vitamin C, the other half were given nothing. The participants who had asked to take the supplement experienced significantly less stress, as measured by their levels of cortisol (a stress hormone), and blood pressure.

Even though it is popular to take vitamins in supplement form, especially vitamin C, I would highly recommend trying to add this stress buster into your diet through whole fruits and vegetables. There are complex interactions occurring inside the fruit between nutrients, vitamins, and other micro-nutrients. Our scientific understanding of these interactions is at a basic level. There is no firm evidence to suggest that isolating any one of these micro-nutrients has any benefits.

In his ground breaking research and subsequent book, *The China Study*, T. Colin Campbell says, "Everything in food works together to create health or disease. The more we think that a single chemical characterizes a whole food, the more we stray into idiocy".

Other Benefits of Eating Fruit

1. Fruit is convenient. You just buy, wash or peel, and eat.

2. Fruit provides plenty of the essential fiber you need for a healthy digestive system.

3. Fruit is generally low in calories.

4. Eating fruit is linked to much lower incidence of the more common diseases in our society, including heart disease, cancer, and diabetes.

5. Fruits which are rich in potassium, such as bananas or oranges, can reduce your blood pressure.

What to Do

Here are some ways of getting more fruit into your diet.

1. Drink more smoothies or shakes. We'll talk about this in a later section.

2. Bring a piece of fruit with you when you're on the go, it makes an ideal fast food. Add some nuts and a bit of celery for the full package.

3. Create a healthy home by keeping sweets out and replacing them with fresh healthy fruits.

*https://www.psychologytoday.com/articles/200304/vitamin-c-stress-buster

25. Eat Your Veggies, Don't Become One!

Root veggies are relatively inexpensive, available throughout the year, and are the most under-appreciated form of great nutrition. Every root vegetable you can think of is packed with fiber and complex carbohydrates. They are also packed with magnesium, vitamin C, and potassium.

Root veggies, like their tree-growing fruity cousins, provide a great energy source which not only lowers your blood sugar levels but can also help your body produce those all-important feel good hormones. Root veggies are also an excellent alternative to those who can't eat whole grains.

Many people are nervous of eating too many carbohydrates, thinking if they eat too many potatoes, they will pile on the pounds and won't be able to fit into their jeans any more. This is absolute nonsense. Eating complex carbohydrates is not the problem. The issue is with what we add to these whole foods to make them taste good. We get fat when we add butter and cream to potatoes, when we top them with cheese, or when we deep fat fry them in oil.

A study conducted way back in the 1920's took a man and a woman and fed them on nothing but potatoes for almost 6 months. The only addition to the diet was a bit of lard and butter to prevent the volunteers from losing weight. The woman was sedentary but the man was an athlete. The investigators said, "The digestion was excellent throughout the experiment and both subjects felt very well. They did not tire of the uniform potato diet and there was no craving for change".

Vegetables in general are your friends. They are packed with everything you need to be physically and mentally fueled-up for life. When you eat rubbish carbohydrates, the type you will find in most processed foods, you're not only putting garbage into your body, you won't have the necessary physical energy to get up and burn those extra calories off. Nor will you have the mental strength it takes to push yourself to do it.

What to Do

There are many ways to cook and serve root veggies.

1. You can simply boil them in a stew, steam them, or roast them in the oven - which is my favorite. I like to get a mixture of root veggies like potatoes, carrots, and beets, mix them up with onions and garlic, a small drizzle of olive oil, a quick turn of sea salt and cracked pepper. I ramp the oven up to full blast and bake until they're done. This usually takes about thirty minutes, depending on how thick you cut the veggies.

2. You can juice any type of vegetables, depending on the quality of your juicer.

26. No Water, No Life

Our bodies and brains are made of 75% water. Even your bones are about 22% water. Your blood has a higher concentration, at 83% with your liver clocking in at a huge 96%. It's no wonder the liver is capable of regenerating itself.

Water is needed for so many essential processes in your body. It protects your organs. It regulates your body temperature. It carries oxygen and nutrients to your cells. Water also helps to absorb those nutrients and aid your metabolism. It plays a crucial role in detoxifying your system. And it moisturizes and protects your joints.

You don't need to be completely dehydrated for things to start going wrong. If your body is a mere half liter under-hydrated you'll feel more stressed, have more headaches, and just feel less energetic in general. The main reason is because dehydration destabilizes your core thermostat.

As dehydration sets in, your blood volume reduces, the blood flow to your skin decreases, which reduces the efficiency of your skin in regulating body temperature, and your body's core temperature rises, reducing it's ability to dissipate heat.

What to Do

1. Start your day off hydrated. First thing in the morning, make it a ritual to drink at least half a liter of water before you do anything else. Leave a glass and bottle of water beside the sink in your bathroom or next to your coffee maker - any place you can't ignore it. If you don't like cold water, warm it a touch by adding some hot water from the kettle. You can also add a slice of lemon

to boost your vitamin C and add a zing to the water.

2. Drink a glass of water before you sit for your meal. It's easy for your body to mistake thirst for hunger. By drinking a glass of water before you sit for your meal, you will only be eating for hunger, not to cure your thirst.

3. Eat more fresh fruit and veggies. Fresh fruit and vegetables are not only packed with nutrients, vitamins, and all that other micro-nutrient goodness, they are also loaded with water. Keep fully hydrated by ordering a salad and some fruit for your lunch. If you find fruit and veg hard to swallow, why not try some fresh juices which we'll talk about in the next section.

27. Fluid, Fruity, and Refreshing

Fresh juice will keep you hydrated, but there's way more to it than that. I love eating fruit and veg, but I sometimes find it hard to fit it all in. All that chewing and grinding just seems to take forever and makes my jaw ache. So I bought a juicer and a couple of books with a lot of juicing recipes. I've got the best of both worlds, I can get all the goodness from the raw fruit and veg into my system without all the hassle of actually grinding it up.

Fresh fruit and vegetables are your prime source of natural macro and micro nutrients, such as the magnesium, vitamin B, Zinc, Potassium, and vitamin C. Once you cook these ingredients, they begin losing some of the nutrition. The higher the heat and the longer you cook for, the more nutrients are lost.

Eating raw fruit is easy. Raw veg can be tough. By juicing the fruit and veg, you get the benefit of all those valuable nutrients but without the hassle and time of cooking and chewing. You lose about 20% of the nutritional value into the pulp, but all is not lost. You can still use the pulp in your soups, stews, curries, and burgers. Or you can throw it onto your compost heap which can help you grow more veg and keep the cycle flowing.

What to Do

1. Buy a juicer that suits what you want to juice. If you only want to make fruit juices, you'll only need a cheap juicer. If you to experiment with tougher veggies, like carrots, potatoes, or turnip, you're going to need to invest in a more durable machine.

2. When making juices, stick to the 80/20 rule. 80% vegetables and 20% fruit.

3. Buy a juicing recipe book to get you started. Alternatively, there are thousands of juicing recipes on the internet.

4. Wash all the produce before use.

5. To save time, prepare your ingredients the night before. Wash everything and place in a container in your fridge, ready to go in the morning.

28. Alcohol: the Destructor

Alcohol has no beneficial effects for your body, mood, emotions, or life. Alcohol is a toxic chemical which you force onto your body for the sake of the illusion of comfort. There is no relief from stress with alcohol, only a temporary reprieve. As far as your problems are concerned, and the stress and anxiety that accompanies these problems, they will all still be there the next morning. Not only that, they'll seem worse because you now have a hangover to contend with. The more you drink to escape yourself, the more you will come around the next morning with your problems being ever so much worse than the night before. And every time you drink alcohol believing that you are relieving your stress, you reinforce this short-term gratification remedy in your mind, which leads to a self-inflicted downward spiral. It's easier to turn to the bottle the next time you feel stressed, and the next time, and the time after that. The real problems behind your stress are not being dealt with, and you get stuck in a vicious circle.

What to Do

1. Don't drink alcohol or take any other drugs. There's nothing to be gained and everything to lose.

2. This book is all about choosing alternatives to alcohol for relaxation, stress relief, or coping with life. If you need help quitting drinking, see my other books *How to Stop Drinking Alcohol* and *Alcohol Freedom*.

3. Visit AlcoholMastery.com for lots of free videos, posts, and thousands of helpful comments from people who are in the same

position as you.

4. Watch this free video on my thoughts about what alcohol does once you put it into your body.
 http://alcoholmastery.com/an-interpretation-of-a-lifetime-of-drunkenness-from-the-other-side/

29. Caffeine. The Gateway Drug?

Is coffee good or bad for you? Just as in alcohol research, information about the health benefits of coffee is sketchy at best. In almost all cases, the results of any research are couched around terms like 'may help prevent...', 'could be responsible for...', 'might', 'could possibly...' and so on. Where is the truth?

Caffeine increases your levels of dopamine and adrenaline, which give you a temporary pop in energy levels, helping you to feel momentarily good. Unfortunately, as in the case of sugar, this boost is always accompanied by a corresponding dip in energy and feelings.

One study about caffeine use, conducted at Duke University Medical Center, found that the effects of drinking coffee in the morning remained active until bedtime and beyond. The researchers also found that caffeine caused stress to increase in people who drank it every day. Professor James D. Lane, Ph.D., says, "The effects of coffee drinking are long-lasting and exaggerate the stress response both in terms of the body's physiological response in blood pressure elevations and stress hormone levels, but it also magnifies a person's perception of stress." Caffeine has a compounding effect both physiologically and psychologically. "The caffeine we drink enhances the effects of the stresses we experience, so if we have a stressful job, drinking coffee makes our body respond more to the ordinary stresses we experience," he said. "The combination of stress and caffeine has a multiplying, or synergistically negative effect."

What to Do

1. Avoid coffee, especially in the first few days of your quit.

2. In the long run, try to find an alternative to caffeinated drinks, one that won't set your body up for such emotional highs and lows.

3. Try a few days without and see how you feel. If you are stressed out, take a break from caffeine for a while. If you start to feel better without the coffee, stick with it.

4. Think about the long-term effect of drinking coffee. Like alcohol, it's not the one cup of coffee that you drink today which does the damage, it's more the accumulative effects of coffee drinking day after day over many years.

30. Soda Pressing!

Truth is, regardless of which type of soda you choose to drink, it's not good for you. The regular version contains far too much sugar and the non-sugar version has way too many chemicals. These drinks have lots of empty calories, no nutritional value, and their long term use will contribute significantly to your bad health, bad moods, and bad life.

Soda increases your risk of heart disease. Even if you only drink one can of soda a day, you increase your risk of having a heart attack over the next 22 years, according to research undertaken by the Harvard School of Public Health.

Another study, published in the European Journal of Nutrition, June 2012 led by Dr Hans-Peter Kubis at the University of Bangor in North Wales found that drinking sugary sodas can not only cause weight gain, it can change your whole metabolism, which can trigger other health problems.

Dr. Kubis explains, "This study proves that our concerns over sugary drinks have been correct. Not only can regular sugar intake acutely change our body metabolism; in fact it seems that our muscles are able to sense the sugars and make our metabolism more inefficient, not only in the present but in the future as well. This will lead to a reduced ability to burn fat and to fat gain. Moreover, it will make it more difficult for our body to cope with rises in blood sugar. What is clear here is that our body adjusts to regular soft drink consumption and prepares itself for the future diet by changing muscle metabolism via altered gene activity – encouraging unhealthy adaptations similar to those seen in people with obesity problems and type 2 diabetes."

He concludes, "Together with our findings about how drinking soft drinks dulls the perception of sweetness, our new results give a stark warning against regularly drinking sugar sweetened drinks"

And the non-sugary versions, well they're no better.

Choosing a diet soda over a regular soda will save you around 140 empty calories, or 39 grams of sugar (just over 9 teaspoons). The price for this sugar saving is a lot of unnecessary chemicals which are just as bad, being linked with a host of diseases.

One study found that older adults who drank diet sodas, because they were concerned about their overall weight, were 44% more likely to have a heart attack. *The Sugar Detox* author, Brooke Alpert says, "Artificial sweeteners trigger insulin, which sends your body into fat storage mode and leads to weight gain". Diet sodas also cause an increased risk of diabetes and metabolic syndrome - high blood pressure, high glucose levels, elevated cholesterol, and an expanding waistline. None of these are very conducive to relaxation.

What to Do

1. If you're thirsty, drink water. This is the most natural drink. Water will keep you hydrated and help your body to relax. Pure water doesn't come with a cocktail of harmful chemicals.

2. If you can't get used to the taste of pure water, add some natural flavorings. Add slices of your favorite fruits, oranges, lemons, watermelon, or apples. Or why not try a slice or cucumber or a sprig of mint.

3. If you want something sweet to drink, try making a fresh juice. One of my favorite recipes is a simple apple and lemon sherbet. All you need for this delicious zingy drink recipe is the juice of two apples and one lemon.

4. Drink green tea. Green tea can help reduce hypertension, it's calorie free, and contains natural antioxidants. You can buy green teas in many different flavors to suit your mood.

5. Try soy milk, especially if you're lactose intolerant. Soy milk is also offered in a wide variety of flavors. Serve ice cold from the fridge.

31. The Solitary Oak Grows the Strongest - The Practice of Solitude

Choosing to be on your own, I don't mean being lonely, but engineering your own deliberate solitude, taking yourself off to a temporary personal retreat, either in reality or in your mind, will help you in so many ways in your life. Solitude lets you recharge your batteries, to grow in strength, and reboot your thinking. It allows you to think more deeply and work through your problems with better precision. A little solitude every so often also improves your focus and efficiency. And finally, taking the time out of your life to focus on yourself helps you to raise the quality of the time you spend with others, enhancing your relationships.

We live in a crowded world where every empty moment tends to be experienced as a void that needs to be filled, at times with absolute nonsense. Being alone in this world, is commonly perceived as something or someone that is missing. Yet, when you consciously and deliberately seek out time on your own, you won't experience loneliness, you are simply an individual unaccompanied.

Loneliness, on the other hand, is completely different to solitude. It is involuntary. The lonely person does not want to be alone, they crave company. Mother Teresa said, "Loneliness and the feeling of being unwanted is the most terrible poverty."

Solitude is about independence, having the time to think, to truly think, without the sonic booms of modern life. Solitude is about getting to know yourself that bit better.

Finding some "me" time lets you to explore yourself without

unnecessary interruption. It gives you the opportunity to be completely self-aware. Solitude is the necessary opposite of intimacy. Paul Tillich, in *The Eternal Now*, said "Our language has wisely sensed the two sides of being alone. It has created the word "loneliness" to express the pain of being alone. And it has created the word "solitude" to express the glory of being alone."

What to Do

Henry Thoreau said, "As you simplify your life, the laws of the universe will be simpler; solitude will not be solitude, poverty will not be poverty, nor weakness." You don't have to take yourself off into the wilderness for months on end, as Thoreau did, you can take small planned chunks of solitude sprinkled through your week.

There's a time for being with people and a time for being with yourself. I love both. For me, there are few things as rewarding as getting lost in a good book or sitting at a street cafe watching the world go by. I become immersed in the narrative spinning out in my head as I read someone else's thoughts or in the brief encounters with people flitting in and out of my life as I sip my coffee. I often find myself in the same meditative state as I walk alone, a place I difficult to come across during standard meditation.

1. First, find a simple space. Your space could be anywhere. You might have a spare bedroom or an office, somewhere you can close the door and get away from it all. If you don't have a room, find a cupboard, anywhere.

2. Turn off the stream. Make sure you have no distractions. Turn off all mobile phones, internet, television, radio, and any other sources of distraction that you control.

3. Use Headphones. If you can't find the space for splendid isolation without the distraction of noises from your normal life, use a pair of headphones. A trick I've found works for me is to use a set of cheap over-the-ear headphones. Through these, I play some soft meditational-type music. At the same time, I use soft foam earplugs in each ear. This does the double job of blocking out

the sound of the outside while helping me to focus on my thoughts, a book, or the music.

4. Go Outdoors. Go for a walk. Sit under a tree in a park. Meditate. You'll always be able to find some place where you can practice your solitude if you venture out of doors.

5. Don't discount finding solitude among others. Taking your dog for a walk might not be sticking to the core idea of being alone, but a dog can make a great solitude partner. Most dogs are content to just be with you, they experiencing their world as you go about experiencing yours. Or you can find anonymous solitude in a crowd of strangers, at the shopping mall for instance.

6. What should you think about? It's your time to think, so think what you want. It really doesn't matter the subject. The most important element is connecting with yourself, in whatever shape or form that takes. Like any form of meditation, the idea is briefly connecting with yourself and disconnecting from everything else.

32. Finding Your Zen Zone

Your personal Zen Zone is somewhere you can take yourself to when things are getting on top. Relaxation is part mind, part body, and part environment. Your Zen Zone is a place that can be used for meditation, solitude time, chilling, personal therapy, or whatever else you need it for. The emphasis is on you, on your own, and relaxation. Your Zen Zone can be a part of your home, your garden, or sitting under a tall, strong tree on a hill overlooking a lush green meadow.

When I was a child, I often visited my Granddad on his allotment in London. This allotment was a patch of ground which he leased from the local council. It was part of an area that had been set aside the purpose, with probably 40 or 50 such allotments on the one piece of land. Anyway, it was my Granddad's place, the place he grew veg, fruit, and herbs. I can't remember how big it was, in my child's eye it looked huge. Looking back, I'd say it must have been about a hundred meters square. It was set out in a long rectangle down the side of a gently sloping hill.

At the top of his plot of land, my Granddad had built a wooden shed with a large window facing out over his little kingdom. Inside, pushed up against the window, was a wooden table and a single old worn armchair. White painted timber shelves lined two of the walls. On these were stacked lots of plant pots, a collection of tools, and various bits and bobs. Whenever he took me up there, he'd always have some hidden goodies stashed away in his rucksack for when 'our' work was finished. When it came to the work, I was more of a hindrance than a help, I'm afraid, but I just loved being with him. He'd bought me a little spade which I used to dig holes, usually in places where they weren't needed, thinking if I dug far enough I could reach China.

Once we were finished with the work, and it was time for lunch, he'd turn a wooden crate upside down and put a cushion on top of it for me to sit on. Then he'd pour a cup of lemonade for me and some tea from a tartan flask for himself. Now came the good stuff. He'd dig around in the bottom of his rucksack for this old round French biscuit tin with a romantic painting of a woman in a green dress who was sitting under the shade of an apple tree, reading a book. This is where my Nan always packed our lunches for the day. You never knew what was going to be hidden inside. I'm not sure he did. As he pulled back the lid, it could be slices from one of my Nan's homemade fruit cakes, ham and cheese sandwiches, pieces of pork pie, or fairy cakes in little paper wrappers. Whatever it was, the food was always accompanied by these deep red paper napkins which served as plates. That's one of my best childhood memories, my Granddad giving me a piece of cake wrapped in a red paper napkin with a big grin on his face, then we'd sit there as happy as larks, looking out over the kingdom.

Thinking back on it now, I wonder how many hours he spent up there in his own in silent contemplation. He had a garden at the back of his house, but that was full of flowers for my Nan. The allotment was his Zen Zone, his place to escape the pressures of life, to gaze over the fruits of his labor and ponder the mysteries of the universe. I think we could all do with such an allotment.

What to Do

1. Choose an area that's isolated from other areas in your home. Alternatively, find somewhere outside your home where you know you won't be disturbed. Find your own allotment.

2. Let everyone know this is your space and time for relaxation.

3. Eliminate any clutter.

4. Fill your area with your relaxation tools. That could be scented candles, incense sticks, a yoga mat, a music player, or just

a comfy armchair for your own silent contemplations. It could be plant pots and trowels.

5. Get comfortable, whatever that looks like to you. Sit loosely with a straight back. Lie flat on your back with uncrossed legs and arms. Lie on your side, curled up in the fetal position. Sit in an old worn-out armchair overlooking your garden. Whatever works for you!

6. Relax and enjoy.

33. Meditating Naked

Naked meditation might strike you as being a bit over-the-top or at least a bit strange. But don't knock it. We're naked coming into this world and it's still the most natural state to be in, regardless our chaste society. Fair enough, nakedness in public is one thing, but getting into the nip in the privacy of your own company is another entirely.

One of the main reasons for practicing regular meditation is to find something inside yourself, an inner peace, and a physical relaxation that can relieve your stress and enable you to handle the cravings of your life. Naked meditation is a symbolic escape from the trappings of our modern society, eliminating everything but the simplistic version of who you are. It can sometimes be easy to get caught up in what we own and the clothes we wear, hiding ourselves behind such superficial trappings. Naked meditation is more than just getting into the nude while you meditate, it's about taking meditation down to its most basic level. It's just you, your body, and your mind.

Because most of us don't feel comfortable being in the nude, naked meditation will seem a bit strange and you may be uncomfortable at first. Even the thought of sitting in the nude with your eyes closed can be slightly unnerving. You may even have feelings that almost border on guilt or shame, of vulnerability, getting caught, or that you're just being silly. But you'll soon overcome all these artificial barriers. When you practice for a time, those feeling will just fade away.

What you'll get from naked meditation is a great sense of connection with the world around you. It's one of the best ways of truly discovering who you really are, without all the superfluous extras. Naked meditation is not meant to be erotic. Being naked while calmly breathing in and out, allowing your mind and spirit wonder, is meant to bring you to an understanding of your 'oneness with the universe', or at least your surroundings, who you really are in the world. It's about pulling back another freedom for yourself, restoring your flexibility to indulge in you as an individual being. It sounds all 'new worldly' but it's not, it's really a simple method of taking yourself back to the basics in life.

What to Do

1. One of the most important things is to be relaxed and comfortable in the knowledge that you are not going to be disturbed. That means having a quiet spot in your home where you can find solitude. Lock the door or make sure you have the house to yourself. If it's too cold, turn on the heating. If it's too hot, turn on a fan or the air conditioning.

2. Dismiss any negative thoughts about what you are doing or why you are doing it. Nakedness is a very natural state to be in, we've just forgotten how. Nudity is a return to innocence.

3. Disrobe and seat yourself ready for meditation.

4. Use the thoughts or feelings of discomfort, vulnerability, or shame to your advantage. Use them to control your meditation. You are about to get to know yourself a little bit better.

5. Breathe deeply. Concentrate on taking long, deep breathes, hold for a second or two at the top of each breath. Now concentrate on the long, slow exhale, holding again for a couple of seconds at the bottom. You are finding relaxation and becoming centered.

6. Feel your body. The coolness or warmth of the air on your skin.

7. Once you are completely relaxed with this feeling of being naked, it's time to turn your reflections inward to your deeper thoughts and feelings.

34. The Ten Tigers of Breathing

There's an old Chinese proverb that says "If you know the art of breathing you have the strength, wisdom, and courage of ten tigers."

One of the best ways of combating stress and bringing about relaxation is through controlling your breathing. You breathe as part of being alive, that's true. But the type of breathing I'm talking about is deliberate breathing to achieve a specific goal condition. When we breathe, we do so for different purposes. You can use your breathing to psyche yourself up before going into an undesirable meeting or facing a tough challenge. You can use breathing to get your brain ready for creative thought, to ward off the nasty colds and flus that are going around in your neighborhood, or as an effective treatment for asthma.

In his book, *The Relaxation Response*, Herbert Benson writes about teaching long, slow breathing to his patients in a Boston hospital. It involves simple deep breathing, in and out, for a period of twenty minutes every day. Dr. Benson's technique consistently reduced the high blood pressure in his patients and the medication that they needed to take.

To find the relaxation response that Dr. Benson writes about will take practice and patience. It won't happen overnight. For some practitioners, it might take a couple of weeks, for others a couple of months. The relaxation response will happen for you if you stick with it. When you habitualize this breathing practice every day, you'll notice yourself feeling more relaxed, not only during your breathing practice, but throughout the rest of your day. This is powerful stuff. It's free. It's simple. You don't need any equipment other than what you were born with. Anyone can do it. You can do it.

Breathing for relaxation can be done anywhere. You don't have to be sat in a meditation pose or dressed in a certain type of clothing. You can practice relaxation breathing while you're sat on a train on your way home from work, stuck in a traffic jam as everyone else is hammering on their car horns, or while you're waiting in a line at the grocery store checkout. Of course, it's better if you're comfortable while you practice your breathing exercises. The more relaxed you are when you start to practice, the quicker you'll get to the place you want to be. Sometimes just calming down is enough.

Depending on your desired outcome, there are many relaxation exercises that you can try. The one I am going describe is very straightforward and can be done anywhere.

What to Do

1. As with all relaxation exercises, first you need to be comfortable. You can sit in a chair, on the floor with a cushion under your butt, or just get as comfortable as you can on the train ride home. Sit tall with your back straight and your belly tucked in or lay flat on your back with your arms and legs stretched out.

2. Close your eyes and start taking slow breathes through your nose.

3. Inhale each breath for the count of three. Hold each breath at the top for a two count. Let it go, breathe out for the count of four or five. At the bottom of each breathe, hold for a count of two.

4. Repeat this sequence for at least 5 minutes.

5. You can adjust the length of each breath, increasing or decreasing the seconds of inhale and exhale until you're comfortable. You can do the same for the amount of time you hold your breath at the bottom and the top. Always breathe longer on the exhale than the inhale.

35. Blow Up Some Balloons

Another form of finding relaxation through breathing is by blowing up balloons. Sound silly? Well it is, sort of.

It works in the first place because it forces you to take long deep breaths. Blowing enough air into the balloon to get it to expand, you first have to take a huge gulp of air into your lungs, expanding your chest to its full capacity. Then you've got to muscle that air out from your lungs and into the balloon.

Second, the act of this deep inhalation and exhalation forces you to take more deliberate, slow breathes in between the big gulps as you try to catch your breath again.

Both these types of breathing engage the parasympathetic system. This is the opposite system that's engaged during the flight or fight response, which is known as the sympathetic nervous system.

The parasympathetic nervous system creates a calmness in your mind and body once the perceived danger of being eaten has gladly passed. The physical and emotional responses that you feel being triggered are known as the rest and digest responses. Your blood pressure decreases, your pulse slows right down, your digestion restarts, your blood sugar levels decrease, and you go into energy saving mode. Everything returns to peace and tranquility!

Blowing up a balloon also invokes a lot of very positive imagery. We associate balloons with children's parties, with fun and laughter, and just the act of blowing up balloon can transport you back to the carefree days of your youth.

What to Do

Choose one of the two techniques below:

1. Strongly exhale into a balloon until you're out of breath. Hold for five seconds. Then inhale slowly through your nose. Repeat a few times. Use this exercise when you are feeling flustered. It will calm and soothe, bringing your breathing under control.

2. After you've done the first exercise a few times and you feel relaxed, you can use the balloon for a different purpose. Blow up the balloon for the final time and tie off the end. Take a marker and write a few words on the balloon. Write a few words about something that is causing you to feel stress. You can write a problem, a person's name, a place, whatever. It could be a feeling about yourself. For instance, "No willpower", "I don't feel good about myself", "I don't think I can do this". Here's the best part. Once you've chosen and written your stress-causing word or phrase on the balloon, you're going to pop it and the word or phrase will burst with it. You pop the balloon using a pencil, scissors, penknife, your fingers, or just stamp on the balloon until it bursts. Before you pop the balloon, think about what you've written on its surface for a few seconds, hold the image of the person or thing in your head. Understand that once you break the balloon, you will be bursting the idea, sending it away with a bang.

I have some more stress popping solutions involving balloons later in this book.

36. Yoga - The Science of the Here and Now

Many people, both men and women, are turning to yoga in their search for answers to the stress problems that they find in this agitated modern-world of ours.

Yoga has been around for over 5,000 years, so there's nothing new about it. There are many types of yoga to suit all ages and abilities. Some modern yoga classes are designed primarily for exercise, increasing your heart rate and getting your sweat glands pumping. Other yoga styles offer insights into calmness, inner strength, and relaxation.

Yoga for relaxation is about releasing physical and mental tension, and learning how to maintain that peacefulness once you have found it. When your body and mind are tense and wound-up, much of your energy is wasted, meaning it's no longer available for the more important things in your life.

Yoga trains your muscles to relax, first consciously, then, after a lot of practice, subconsciously. As you progress through your yoga training, you will find your overall energy levels improving and lasting longer throughout the day.

The benefits of regular yoga workouts don't stop there. As well as strengthening your body, yoga exercises can help you to develop your mental stamina. Although the average human brain weighs only 3 pounds, about 2% of your overall bodyweight, it uses 20% of the body's energy. So it's important you train your body and your mind to conserve this energy through relaxation.

I've always thought that yoga was for women. Then, once I quit drinking, I was searching around for a spiritual release as well as a physical one. I found some local classes in Kundalini Yoga. Although the classes were held in Spanish, and my skills in the language weren't that great at the time, I enrolled for two sessions a week. It was one of the best things I've ever done. The classes were held in a purpose-built one-room school, set into some local pine woodland. In the winter we practiced indoors and then took everything outside under the sun during the spring and summer. Meditating with the morning sun on your back and birdsong in your ears just adds to the whole spiritual buzz.

I don't go to the classes any more, although I'm thinking of returning, but I continue to practice meditation and Kundalini at least three times a week at home in my Zen Zone. It has become a part of my routine, a welcome addiction in my life.

I also broke another of one my life preconceptions, yoga is not just for women. Once a yoga class gets under way, everyone is the same, we're all as sweaty and ugly as hell. Nobody laughed at my inability to stretch or bend or hold a pose for longer than a couple of seconds before toppling like a toddler learning how to walk. So for any men out there, get over yourself. This is an all-round exercise method that does wonders for the body, the mind, and the spirit.

What to Do

Before I tell you one of my favorite yoga relaxation poses, here are some tips on getting the most out of your yoga sessions.

1. Find a quiet place where you are unlikely to be disturbed.

2. Keep yourself warm. Maintain a nice temperature in the room, use a blanket for static yoga poses, and lay on a mat to keep yourself off the floor.

3. Use a pillow under your head and another under your knees for support when you go into reclining postures.

4. Don't practice yoga on a full stomach. If you need some energy before starting, have a small piece of fruit or a glass of fruit

juice.

Now here's my favorite pose.

Shavasana: Deep Relaxation

Shavasana, or Corpse Pose, aids the body's natural rejuvenating and healing processes. It involves just laying down, which is why I like it so much.

1. Lay on your back with your legs 12 - 18 inches apart. Place a small pillow under your head, supporting the natural arch of your neck. Your arms should be naturally relaxed by your sides. Your hands should be in a comfortable position, preferably palms facing upwards and your fingers relaxed.

2. Close your eyes.

3. Create a relaxing picture in your mind. Your internal images are about building your intention to relax. Most people find it easy to imagine a peaceful scene in their minds. Try thinking about lying on a beach, hearing the sound of the water lapping against the shore and the gentle breeze blowing over your body.

4. Begin breathing slowly and deeply. Breathe out slightly longer that you breathe in, hold at both the top and bottom of each breath for a second or two.

5. Now I want you to tension your muscles, one by one. Start with your feet. Tense the muscles in your foot, hold for a couple of seconds and relax. Do this once more. Now move to your calf muscles. Put tension on your calf muscles, hold for a couple of seconds, and release. Continue with the same tensioning and releasing sequence as you move up your body, tensing and relaxing the muscles in your thighs, bottom, stomach, chest, and back. Then tense and release the muscles in your hands, forearms, biceps and triceps, shoulder, neck, and finally the muscles in your face. Always follow the same sequence. Tense the muscles, hold for two seconds and release, repeat once more.

6. Just allow your breathing to relax without exerting too much control. Be aware of your thoughts, but don't pay them too much attention. When they come, just hold them for a second and

then let them go. Gently bring your thoughts back to your breathing and your relaxed body. Be conscious of your body loosening and unwinding. If you feel tautness, let it go. Pay attention to every part of your body. Often you will notice tension around the eyes or jaw. Just release that tension and allow it to drift away.

7. As you come to the end of your Shavasana session, keep the intention in your mind that you will remain relaxed. Say to yourself that you are going to carry this relaxed state with you throughout the rest of your day.

8. Before opening your eyes, gently stretch your arms above your head. At the same time, gently stretch your legs out.

9. Open your eyes slowly. Sit up slowly. Relax!

37. Happiness is an Inside Job - The Magic of a Smile

A smile is the light in your window that tells others that there is a caring, sharing person inside.

Denis Waitley

Smile, it's free therapy.

Douglas Horton

Smile

Smile though your heart is aching

Smile even though it's breaking

When there are clouds in the sky, you'll get by

If you smile through your fear and sorrow

Smile and maybe tomorrow

You'll see the sun come shining through for you

Light up your face with gladness

Hide every trace of sadness

Although a tear may be ever so near

That's the time you must keep on trying

Smile, what's the use of crying?

You'll find that life is still worthwhile, if you just smile

That's the time you must keep on trying

Smile, what's the use of crying?

You'll find that life is still worthwhile, if you just smile

Charlie Chaplin

Telling a person to smile when they're in the middle of some trouble or anxiety might not be the best advice to offer, especially if they're in a bad mood. But if you can fire that advice in your own direction, during your own times of stress, if you can bring a smile to your own face and keep it there despite the clouds in the sky, the chances are you'll make yourself feel better for doing it. Just the simple act of smiling when you're stressed out can make you feel better, even if you don't really mean it. It's another example of you being in control when you might not think you are. It's your choice to smile or not. It's your choice to change your mood or not!

Smiling is such a natural thing for us humans to do. It's one of the first things a new-born baby learns from their mum and dad. It's an inbuilt talent. We're excellent judges when it comes to telling if someone is genuine when they smile. There is something buried deep within each that lets us know immediately if someone is faking a smile. It just doesn't look right. This is a vital form of self-defense. The lips might be drawn back in the correct way, all the teeth are showing in what looks like a proper smile, but there's something about the eyes and the rest of the face that gives away the insincerity and possibly the danger. We know it as a wolf in sheep's clothing.

Fortunately, we can override that ability when it comes to fooling ourselves with our own smiles.

Even the simple trick of holding a pencil between your teeth can fool your brain into releasing a little feel-good juice. In 1988, participants of a study* were asked to put a pencil between their teeth and forcing a smile while they rated cartoons for humor. Those who forced themselves to smile rated the cartoon as funnier than those who didn't use the pencil trick. Try it and see for yourself.

What to Do

1. When you are feeling stressed or you need to relax, force yourself to smile. If you need to pop a pencil or a chopstick between your teeth to force yourself into a parody of a smile, this is a good start. Your brain will respond. Better still, try to include your eyes in your smile, bringing in the muscles of your whole face.

2. Sarah Pressman, who has researched the link between smiling and building happiness says "The next time you are stuck in traffic or are experiencing some other type of stress you might try to hold your face in a smile for a moment. Not only will it help you 'grin and bear it' psychologically, but it might actually help your heart health as well."

3. Play a happy song or read some funny lyrics or jokes while you pull a big smile.

*http://www.ncbi.nlm.nih.gov/pubmed?term=Strack%2C%2 0Martin%20%26%20Stepper%20back%20in%201988%20%28I nhibiting%20and%20facilitating%20conditions%20of%20the%2 0human%20smile

38. The Serious Benefits of Laughter Yoga

A day without laughter is a day wasted.

Charlie Chaplin

Through humor, you can soften some of the worst blows that life delivers. And once you find laughter, no matter how painful your situation might be, you can survive it.

Bill Cosby

Laughter is an instant vacation.

Milton Berle

There is little success where there is little laughter.

Andrew Carnegie

Laughter is the best medicine. Not unlike smiling, laughing out loud is one of the best antidotes to stress and it can help you to relax your whole body and mind. Genuine laughter boosts your immune system, releases your body's natural feel-good hormone, endorphins, and improves the flow of blood in and around your heart. Laughing also helps to protect you from the dangers of heart attack and cardiovascular disease. It is almost impossible to feel down or depressed at the same time as you are laughing your ass off.

Laughter yoga is based on the belief that forced laughter gives you the same physical and mental benefits as spontaneous laughter. Also known as Hasyayoga, laughter yoga was developed by Dr. Madan Kataria as an exercise routine for a small group of people in a local public park in Mumbai. Now there are more than 8000 Laughter Clubs throughout the world. Dr. Kataria's basic philosophy is that you must laugh every day, even if you don't feel like laughing.

What to Do

The Laughter Club slogan is, 'Fake it until you make it'. Because your body doesn't intellectualize its emotions, it cannot tell the difference between a fake emotion and a real one. Just as you can bring yourself down by acting down, so you can bring yourself up by acting up. The first thing you have to do to get into the mood of laughing is to fake it.

1. Make the sounds of laughter. Ho Ho Ho. Ha Ha Ha. He He He.

2. Play around with the sounds.

3. Play around with your expressions.

4. Pull funny faces and put on funny voices.

When you first try this, you are probably going to feel a little weird. Don't worry. It is a little weird. But it works and it makes you feel good. Once you have practiced fake laughing for some time, you will find it much easier to transform from fake laughing to proper hilarity.

Here's a YouTube video of Dr. Kataria laughing alone at 5am, trying not to make a sound and wake up his entire family. https://www.YouTube.com/watch?v=QvAkyoA7l4U

39. Motion Affects Emotion

The word emotion derives from the latin "emovere", which means "move out". If you examine the word emotion, you'll see that it contains the word motion, which suggests a link between the emotions and physical movement.

In 1884, William James said that first something happens in the world which causes a physical reaction, then we emotionally respond to that action - motion causing emotion.

For example, you are walking alone down a dark street late at night. Suddenly, you become aware that someone's behind you, you hear their footsteps, the sound of their heavy breathing. Your own breathing deepens as you listen intently, trying to isolate the threat. Your heart speeds up and you might begin to tremble.

What are your reactions? First you notice how your body's behaving, then you interpret that behavior as your body preparing itself for the fight or flight response. Only then do you feel the emotion of fear.

James was arguing that without the physical feeling of the emotion, the fear in this case, there would be no emotion. You don't feel it, so it's not there. He said, "We find we have nothing left behind, no 'mind-stuff' out of which the emotion can be constituted, and that a cold and neutral state of intellectual perception is all that remains. ... What kind of an emotion of fear would be left, if the feelings neither of quickened heart-beats nor of shallow breathing, neither of trembling lips nor of weakened limbs, neither of goose-flesh nor of visceral stirrings, were present, it is quite impossible to think. Can one fancy the state of rage and picture no ebullition of it in the chest, no flushing of the face, no dilatation of the nostrils, no clenching of the teeth, no impulse to vigorous action, but in their stead limp muscles, calm breathing, and a placid face?"

Many other theories have been put forward in the intervening years, but I do like the basis for James' theory although it has its flaws and areas where it just doesn't fit. For instance, we often feel an emotion when the cause is not immediately evident - hairs standing on the back of your neck because of a feeling.

The bottom line is that your emotions are there for a reason. Their job is to motivate you into doing something, into taking an action.

In recent years, much research has been focused around discovering a cure for depression. A lot of this research has been concentrated around changing a person's emotions by persuading them to do something. The theory is, you can change the behavior by altering the actions that are attached to it.

There's ample evidence that inaction is one of the leading causes of depression. It's easy to see how this might be so. You experience some disappointments in your life, you pull back a little, isolating yourself, you reduce your positive experiences because you're isolated, this causes you to withdraw some more, and a vicious circle ensues.

So, your emotions are a call to action. They are your body's way of telling you that you need to do something, to respond.

Your emotions are a part of who you are, but more importantly, they are mostly in your control. If you don't believe me, watch a sad movie, look at some photos of a loved one who has passed on, or listen to your favorite comedian. It's not that you're doing these things that causes you to feel sad or happy, it's because you are choosing to do these things and you are continuing to do them beyond the initial emotional response.

For example, you cry about a soppy old movie, some made-up story about a couple in love who are torn apart by the terrors of a war. Despite your 'negative' emotional reaction, you continue to watch. All the while you know it's nor for real, that these characters don't exist, and that their love is a figment of someone else's imagination. But your mind is causing an emotional response as if it *were* real. This is your choice. You are choosing to ignore the sham of what's playing out in front of you and instead focus on the emotions you are feeling as if they were all real. In all good fiction, the words belong to the writer, but the emotional resonance belongs to you, the reader.

Let's take another example. Ask yourself how happy you are, ask: "What have I got in my life to be happy about right now?" Your response could focus on the things in your life that are making you happy. Or you can presume that you have nothing in your life that's making you happy, focusing in on the things you wish were part of your life but are not yet in your life.

Where do you place your focus most of the time? On the positive or on the negative? Remember the good times in your life and you'll likely feel happy. Remember a horrible time and guess how you'll feel?

Getting back to motion affecting emotion, often the best way of responding to anxiety or stress is just to do something, to do anything.

One of my favorite emotional reconditioners is walking.

If I'm feeling tetchy, nervous, or anxious, I know I need to walk. If I haven't been out walking for a while I feel the tension building. Once I've put on my shoes and I'm out in the fresh air, placing one foot in front of the other, my mind relaxes and my body gradually unwinds, releasing all that built-up tension. It doesn't take long before I'm getting into a meditation zone.

For now, let's take a look at what you can do to focus the power of motion into altering your emotions.

What to Do

1. Just do. What you do is up to you, just be sure that you do. Do something that involves movement. Do an activity that gets you up from the couch.

2. Change your environment. Take an action that moves you outside the physical place you're in right now. It's best if you can get outdoors because you get the added bonus of fresh air into your lungs and sunlight on your back.

3. Move away from negativity. I find the older I get the less time I have to suffer fools or negatively oriented people. Don't put up with negative people in your life. Sometimes the negativity might come from a family member, from the closest people in your life. Move away from them. You don't have to make it a permanent move, just enough time to re-balance your thoughts and your mind.

4. Get with other people, especially the positive kind. Smiling is infectious, but so is frowning. Choose the former and you'll feel better about yourself. It's said that you can tell a lot about a person by the five closest people to them. For the most part, these closest people are your choice… choose wisely!

5. Think positive thoughts. It doesn't take any more energy to think a positive thought as it does to think a negative thought. You are much more likely to feel less stressed and more relaxed if you allow yourself to think good thoughts, to see the positive side of any situation. Life is too short for beating yourself up.

6. If you can't focus on positive thoughts, have a positive mantra on standby that you can repeat over and over in your mind. For example, try: "I feel happy", "I love myself", "I'm in a great mood today", "I feel fantastic about my life right now". You fake it until you make it!

Let's look at some examples of motion changing emotions.

40. A Pebble Affecting the Ocean - Moving-on-the-spot

"The least movement is of importance to all nature. The entire ocean is affected by a pebble"

Blaise Pascal

Moving-on-the-spot is any form of exercise that you can do when you don't have time to put in a full workout session, you're restricted by space, or you just want a quick 5 minute pick-me-up in the middle of the day. Performing any moving-on-the-spot exercise is a good way of changing your emotions through motion.

You can move-on-the-spot almost anywhere that you can stand. There are also forms of these exercises you can do while sitting, kneeling, or laying down. So, you'll find plenty of opportunities to exercise-on-the-spot during your day. You might be riding an elevator, peeling some potatoes, watching the TV, even standing waiting for a bus or train. Of course, some exercises might need a bit of privacy, but even waiting in a queue at the grocery store gives you the chance to secretly burn off some excess energy. For instance, stand with your feet together, arms by your side, and lift yourself onto your toes and back down to your heels.

What to Do

Some Public Exercises

Here's some other mini-workouts you can do in public:

Stomach Vacuum

For the stomach vacuum, place your hands on your hips and exhale all the air out of your lungs. Suck in your stomach as much as possible while expanding your chest. Try visualizing your belly-button squeezing towards your spine. Hold this stance for a few seconds. Repeat as many times as you can or want. Do this workout in the office, while working on your computer, while standing in a queue, stuck in traffic, almost anywhere.

Walk

Instead of taking the bus or train to work, walk or cycle. This is the most natural form of exercise you can do in public.

Take the Stairs

If you have a choice of taking the elevator or the stairs, take the stairs every time. If you work on the eightieth floor of a high-rise office building, take the stairs for the first ten flights, then hop onto the elevator for the rest of the journey up.

The Silent Seat Squeeze

How much energy could you be burning by just clenching and unclenching your butt cheeks? To do this exercise, squeeze those puppies together and hold for five to ten seconds, release and repeat. You'll get an uplift in your mood and your bottom.

Some Private Exercises (Or Public if you dare!)

1. Jumping Jacks

2. Marching-on-the-spot

3. Jogging-on-the-spot

4. Squats

5. Leg raises

6. Hoola hoop (with or without the hoop)

7. Deep breathing

8. Tree pose or other yoga balance stance

9. Stationary lunges

10. Shoulder circles

41. No One Can Walk Your Road for You

One of the best ways I know to relax, chill out, reduce the stress, get my brain activated, and generally fire me up, is to take a simple walk. Walking is a cornerstone habit in my life which I hope to continue until the day I die. Here's some reasons I think walking is one of the best possible all round motions to alter your emotions.

- It offers a change of environment.
- It gives you a decent workout.
- You can vary the pace and terrain to suit your needs.
- You can do it anywhere.
- You don't need any fancy equipment, you just get up and go.
- You can substitute walking for your sit-down meditation.

I have tried running, several times in the past, and it's just not for me. At one stage, I could run over 10 kilometers on a treadmill, but I never really enjoyed it. I have never found the buzz that a lot of other people talk about. Plus, every time I ran it caused me too much pain or led to injuries, especially when I ran outdoors. Runners tell me the pain disappears after a while, but I haven't stuck it out long enough to find out. Life's too short to be doing things you don't want or like to do.

Also, I like listening to audiobooks or podcasts while I'm out walking. Or sometimes I just like to hear the slow plod of my feet. It helps me to think, to meditate. This means I can put in an exercise shift and be mentally productive at the same time. This kind of mental productivity is impossible for me while I'm running, I'm always too busy trying to catch my breath.

What to Do

Set yourself a target of a certain number of steps per day. Most people walk about 4,000 steps per day on average. Buy yourself a pedometer and set a target of 7,500 to 10,000 steps. You'll be surprised at how easily you can hit this target.

Here's some tips for getting more walking into your life:

1. Walk to the shops.

2. Take the stairs instead of the elevator.

3. Walk the kids to school, regardless of the weather or the complaints of the young ones. (You're instilling a really positive habit into your kids as well).

4. Get a dog.

And if you find walking boring?

1. Listen to music, audiobooks, podcasts.

2. Find someone to walk with.

3. Join a walking group.

Walking is something you can do for the rest of your life. It won't overly tax your energy. It will help maintain healthy joints and muscles, give you a mental break from your daily routine, help you stay active for longer.

42. Log Off, Shut Down, Go Run

As I said in the last section, running was never one of my favorite activities., but I know plenty of people who swear by it. Horses for courses, I suppose.

Having said that, running is another exercise that's free, you can do it anywhere, and you don't need any specialized equipment, apart from a good pair of trainers.

What to Do

1. Before you begin any strenuous exercise routine, you should pay a quick visit to your doctor, just to be on the safe side, especially if you are over 40.

2. Although you don't need much equipment, you should invest in a quality pair of trainers specifically designed for your foot type. The rest of your outfit is down to you. As a general rule, your clothing should be comfortable, loose fitting, and made from material that won't cause you to sweat too much.

You'll find an informative guide to running footwear here: http://www.runningshoesguru.com/best-running-shoes-wizard/

3. Plan where you're going to run before you leave home. The main hurdle for anyone just getting started in running is to put that first step outside the front door. Know which direction you're going to take and roughly how far you're going to go. You don't have to kill yourself on your first day. Aim for small and steady.

4. Take it easy in the beginning. I always have the urge to do more than I'm capable of. Maybe that's why I make a better walker than a runner. Ease yourself into your routine gradually. Begin

with just five minutes if that's all you can manage. If you feel like doing more after your first five minutes are done, then go for it. If you can't run in the beginning, start out by just walking. Then work your way up to five minutes. Try this sequence: 30 seconds running, 1 minute walking, 30 seconds running, 1 minute walking, 1 minute running, and the final minute walking.

5. Always stretch before you begin each run. Dynamic stretching is the best because it closely mimics the exercise you'll be doing, in this case running. Fast walking, knee lifts, climbing steps, and marching on the spot. These all are good warm-ups as they stretch the specific muscles you'll be using on your run.

6. As I pointed out in step 4, the way to train yourself for endurance and stamina is to run for a set time, then walk for a set time. Run, walk, run, walk. Your objective is to run for longer, walk for less. Eventually, your aim should be to run for a full thirty minutes without stopping.

7. How much should you run? It all depends on what you have in mind. Run as much as you feel like. If you feel stressed, put on your shoes and go out running until you've burned the stress off. If you want to build running into a regular exercise routine, you need to aim for a target, see the last step. This book is about concentrating on reducing stress and increasing relaxation, so run until you've achieved these goals.

43. Appreciating the Good People

"When you see a good person, think of becoming like her/him. When you see someone not so good, reflect on your own weak points."

Confucius

Have you ever sat in a crowded place just watching the world going by? Of course you have, we've all done it; it's a part of our human nature to be curious about our fellow man.

People watching is also another form of meditation. It's about being in the moment and being conscious of what's happening around you.

Of course, to get the benefits of this in-the-momentness, you don't actually have to watch people. You can pull a chair up to your window and watch the clouds drifting across the sky, birds hopping around your back garden, or you can listen to a group kids playing in the distance. You can lay on your couch watching a spider canter up and down the wall, the sun's rays as they play across the room, or just listen to the gentle tick-tock of the old clock in your hallway. But I think we get the most benefits by watching others going about their business while we just observe, sitting on a bench or at an outdoor cafe, sipping a cool juice, not judging, just enjoying.

People watching is more than just curiosity. People watching is a very basic method of self-help. It's how we learn almost everything when we are young. Learning through observation and replication. We observe and ask ourselves basic questions. How do the people in your life behave? How do they deal with certain situations? How would you react under the very same conditions?

We can turn the focus onto ourselves. When you see people behaving in a certain way, speaking in a particular tone of voice, especially if you don't approve of how they're acting or talking, examine your own behavior and the way you sometimes speak or behave. Do you see any similarities? Are there things you see in others that you also see in yourself, things you might not like?

Neuro-Linguistic Programming practitioners employ a technique called modeling. NLP uses modeling to study and attempt to emulate the successes of others. This process begins with carefully watching what the other person is doing. The modeler tries to understand the other persons thought processes, unraveling their skills, values, and beliefs. For instance, if you wanted to become a great golfer, you first find a great golfer that you would like to copy. Then you begin by just observing. You watch what he does and you try to reproduce his stances and behaviors. Then you think about his thought processes, trying to figure out what he's actually thinking and how he feels as proceeds through his swing.

You can adopt a similar approach to emulating people who have already successfully quit drinking. What are they doing with their time? How do they relax? How do they have fun and relieve stress? What do they drink instead of alcohol? Who do they hang out with? How have they altered their thought patterns?

Of course, you can just sit, relax, and watch people going about their day, taking it no further than that.

What to Do

1. Find a comfortable chair. Just sit and watch.

2. Watch people who appear to be relaxed. What are they doing that gives them that appearance? How are they sitting or standing? How are they speaking?

3. How can you apply these things in your own life?

44. The Magic of Tidying Up

"The question of what you want to own is actually the question of how you want to live your life."

Marie Kondo

I recently read a book called The Life Changing Magic Of Tidying Up by Marie Kondo, a Japanese organizing consultant. Her promise in the book is that if you go through your home and systematically tidy, you'll never have to do it again, leaving you with a forever tidy home... Nice!

I bought the book based on a recommendation from a good friend of mine, a man who's not generally known for being the tidiest person on the planet. In fact, when he first recommended this book to me I was a little taken aback. He normally tells me about business books, marketing, management, that kind of thing. He sold it to me as one of the best personal organization books out there. It's a short read, so I bit the bullet and opened it up.

I am a clutter-monster. I have clutter everywhere, or at least I did until I read this book. I tend to store things just in case I might ever need them again. And I store some of the most ridiculous items, old toothbrushes that might 'come in handy' at some future point, old t-shirts that are full of holes but I still use as 'house-clothes, and really nonsensical stuff like old mobile phones that I just can't bear to toss. Why? It just makes no sense.

The problem with physical clutter is it creates life chaos which can lead to lots of overwhelm and stress. Mental clutter can produce a similar type of stress. In Kondo's book, she writes with a lot of respect about the things she is surrounded by. She says that if you hold one of your possessions in your hands and it doesn't spark some sort of joy, you should immediately toss it! She asks, "Are you happy when you hold a piece of clothing that is not comfortable or does not fit? Are you happy to hold a book that does not touch your heart?" If you can't say yes to these questions, the item doesn't belong in your life.

Kondo persuades you to ask what each item has done for you or what lesson has it taught you. For instance, she talks about picking up a piece of clothing you might have bought in the sales. You thought it was a good idea at the time, it was cheap and you were rushed. But when you got it home, you decided that it just wasn't your color or you really didn't like the style after all. You shoved it to the back of your closet and forgot all about it. Her point is that you've learned a valuable lesson about yourself from this piece of clothing. It has deepened your understanding about your style and what colors you really like. She says that you should thank the item for the service it has provided for you, send it on its new journey, perhaps providing a different service to another person. This is a bit strange, but it's an interesting take on how we could regard our possessions.

What to Do

Read the book. Here's a quick rundown of the method.

1. Work through your possessions by category and in the following order: clothing, books, papers, miscellaneous, and mementos.

2. Gather everything in your home from the first category and bring everything to a single place, your front room floor perhaps, making a big pile.

3. Start with your clothing. The reason you start with this category is because your clothing has the least sentimental value for you. On the other hand, your mementos, personal papers, letters, cards, and that type of thing, have a much deeper and personal meaning. So they're more difficult to discard. I've already gone through my clothing. It was enervating. I tossed about 80% of the clothing I owned, taking the discarded stuff either to a charity

shop or the bin if it was too worn.

4. Go through each item and make a quick gut decision. Don't ponder on anything for too long. You're looking for an immediate response to the question, "Does this make me feel happy?"

Tidying around your home is also a great way of getting up and moving, in the spirit of motion changing emotion. You take your mind away from drinking, or whatever habit you're trying to change, onto something much more productive.

45. Vacation Equation: Eat, Relax, Sleep, Repeat

A change of environment is often all it takes to relieve bottled-up pressure. In the first few days of changing any behavior, your old habits will be trying to drag you back into the regular patterns of your old life. These behavior patterns can be triggered by so many different routine things, from the people in your life to your own thoughts.

One of the most powerful triggering areas in your life is your environment. Your home is full of significant things that act as triggers for unwanted routines, like drinking a beer or a glass of wine. One trigger might be the chair you always sit in, the place you used to use for drinking or smoking in the evenings. Or the trigger might be something as simple as the sound of the fridge door opening and closing, reminding you of the beers that used to sit on the shelves.

By taking a vacation, you eliminate virtually all these triggers at once. The people you normally associate with, the streets and bars you usually frequent, and the natural triggers that are all over your home. All of these can be left behind with one swipe of your credit card.

New surroundings offer freshness and vibrancy. A vacation lets you get away from the old routines and from the stress of your daily living. This can work wonders on your levels of perseverance and motivation to kick your habit for good. Of course, there will still be triggers on your vacation, but a lot fewer, making them much easier to handle.

What to Do

1. Think about your past vacations. What did you get up to? Where did you go? If you are anything like me, alcohol was always a big motivator about location and activities once you got to your destination. For me, vacation time meant not having the normal restrictions about when and where I could drink. If I wanted to have a beer for breakfast, for instance, that's just what I'd do. You can learn a lot from understanding your past vacation routines, then choosing to do something completely different.

2. Choose a destination that offers minimum temptations. Make it difficult for yourself to have a drink. Don't go on an all-inclusive booze cruise for instance. Think about going on a retreat or a spa holiday where you can be pampered and destressed. To be honest, it's so nice to go on a vacation and come back not feeling like you need another one.

3. Plan as much about your vacation as you can, before you leave home. Good planning makes for less stress and less likelihood that you'll get bored.

46. Getting into the Flow: Crafting and DIY

Crafting and DIY are two more meditation-like activities that can help you take your mind off things, helping you to destress and relax.

Creativity, in all its many forms, can ease you into a state of flow, which was first described by Mihaly Csikszentmihalyi in his book of the same name. He said, "When we are involved in (creativity), we feel that we are living more fully than during the rest of life. You know that what you need to do is possible to do, even though difficult, and sense of time disappears. You forget yourself. You feel part of something larger."

Clinical neuropsychologist, Catherine Carey Levisay also speaks about the benefits of creativity in all its forms. She says, "There's promising evidence coming out to support what a lot of crafters have known anecdotally for quite some time. And that's that creating -- whether it be through art, music, cooking, quilting, sewing, drawing, photography (or) cake decorating -- is beneficial to us in a number of important ways."

What to Do

1. Select your project. Crafting means any activity or hobby that creates things by hand. DIY is the bigger brother of crafting.

2. Here's a few websites to check out for inspiration:

For DIY

http://www.instructables.com/

http://www.diynetwork.com

http://diylife.co/

http://lifehacker.com/

http://gizmodo.com/

http://makezine.com/

http://www.doityourself.com/

http://greenupgrader.com/

Crafting

http://mybrownpaperpackages.com/

http://www.centsationalgirl.com/

http://www.craft-astrophe.com/

http://makezine.com/craft/

http://dabbled.org/

http://geekcrafts.com/

http://www.howdoesshe.com/

http://mochimochiland.com/

http://pizzazzerie.com/

http://www.craftsy.com/

3. Set aside some quality time for you and your project.

4. Set the mood with lighting, smells, and music.

5. Get into flow!

47. 7 Reasons You Should Turn off Your TV

How much TV do you watch? Do you know? I really didn't have a clue how much TV I was watching until I sat down one day and worked it out.

How much TV did you watch just this week? Work it out.

How many shows did you watch?

How much time did each one take, including the ads?

What about movies?

YouTube?

The average American watches 34 hours per week, according to a Nielson report. That's incredible! And that's only the average. Some people are watching way more.

Why should you cut down? Here's 7 reasons.

1. TV conditions negativity.

The rule of thumb for any TV program is negativity, whether it's the news, drama, even comedies. In the UK, most TV shows are known as programs. The listings for these TV shows, on the BBC, Sky TV, or ITV, for instance, are known as programming. This is not far from the truth. As you stare at the screen your brain is being programed to accept all this negativity.

2. TV creates false perceptions and expectations.

Ask any honest movie or TV star and they'll tell you that the person you see up there on the screen is false, it's just a persona, it's not the truth. This fakery creates a distorted perception in the mind of the watcher, which brings me onto my next point.

3. TV creates feelings of inadequacy about your own life.

Some TV shows create impossible-to-live-up-to expectations for ourselves. They are delusions. When we see these perfect people, their perfect lives, and the perfect settings in which they live, it's very natural to make comparisons with your own life. It doesn't take much for you to draw the conclusion that you and your life are lacking, causing feelings of inadequacy.

4. TV can normalize bad habits and poison your beliefs.

How many references do you see and hear on the Television about alcohol? When you don't see alcohol as a problem, you probably don't notice just how many times every day alcohol is mentioned on your TV in one form or another. This constant flow of propaganda has an influence on your mind. When you see the 'normal' drinking, it reinforces that behavior in as normal.

TV is also full of negative stereotypes - the fat person, the socially inept person, the stupid person. These people are sneered at and are always the butt of jokes.

And the news? What's new about the news? Nothing! It's the same old stuff served up on a different day. It's all about death and destruction, problems and pain. Very rarely is there ever good news. There is plenty of good news in the world; why is that hardly ever reported? Because it doesn't sell newspapers or pay for ad slots.

The news of the world has become a form of gruesome entertainment that taints your perception of life. There will always be another disaster, another death, another form of pain that you can't do anything about. That's life. It's been life from the very beginning. I'm not saying you should ignore what's going on in the world, but be very, very selective about what you allow into your mind.

5. TV is not relaxing.

The best ways of relaxing and releasing stress involve being physically or mentally active or letting yourself go with one form of meditation or another. Watching TV does none of the above. While watching TV, your brain is constantly churning over useless information, processing this information, and more importantly, transforming it into emotional reactions. When you consider that the majority of TV is super-negative, you're sponging up lots of useless crap and converting it into negative energy.

6. TV is addictive.

Just as alcohol and cigarette companies do everything in their power to get you hooked onto their brand of product, the business of TV relies on hooking viewers into watching for as long as possible. It's not about entertainment, it's about money. Providing entertainment is just a means to this monetary end. Think about the anticipation that each network creates when they release a new season of a long running popular show. Or what about the cliffhangers at the end of each soap episode? Think about the never ending cycle of 'breaking news' stories that continually fill our news channels, not to speak of the constant sensationalism.

7. TV wastes your time.

If I asked you to tell me how many days you have in your entire life, how many would you say? Roughly speaking, your four score and ten years on this planet (70 x 365 days) equals 25,550 days, that's it! Not a lot, is it! Given that the average person watches 34 hours of TV in a single week, that adds up to a staggering 5000+ hours of your life... 20%. I never looked at my TV viewing in this way, but after doing my own calculations, I'm going to have to get out of the house more!

What else could you be doing with your time?

What to Do?

1. Do your own calculations about the amount of time you spend watching one form of TV or another over a day, a week, or a year.

2. Turn off the TV or at least cut down on your viewing times.

3. Like any other change in your life, this is going to take time,

you will feel uncomfortable for a while, but if you persevere you'll find much more productive things to do with yourself, your family, and your friends.

48. May the Forest be With You - The Magic of Shinrin-Yoku

"The clearest way into the universe is through the forest wilderness."

John Muir

If you're a hiker or nature lover, you already know the benefits of getting out into the 'wilderness', communing with nature. Forest bathing is the practice of slow walking or sitting in a forest. The Japanese call it Shinrin-yoku (森林-よく). Forest bathing involves absorbing the unique environment that forestry and woodlands have to offer. You practice shinrin-yoku by walking or sitting under the leafy canopy, breathing the high-oxygen air, inhaling the scents of the forest, the sights, the sounds, and the blissful atmosphere.

I love woods, trees, and the complete solitude that you can really only find in the middle of a forest. I think it has something to do with my introverted nature. I worked for many years in and around the forests of Ireland. For the most part, the daily work was as far away from the tranquil forest bathing world. Instead, I was surrounded by the sounds and smells of machinery, chainsaws, timber extractors, and felling equipment. Not very nice!

But every so often, usually when I was scouting deep into the heart of the woods, I'd find that harmonious Shangri-La place that always gave me the sense that the job was worthwhile after all. Without another soul around, it was a chance to experience life as it must have been lived for thousands of years before the cities and factories were ever thought of. It was just me and nature. I'd take out for my lunch, open a flask of tea and eat a sandwich while sitting on the soft, pine needle covered ground with my back resting against a tree. I loved that friendly peace, the sounds of the birds and other woodland creatures scurrying about their daily business.

Woodlands are always filled with wonderful aromas of sap, bark, pine needles, leaves, moss, and the like, all being carried along on huge waves of life-giving oxygen. There's also this strange feeling of safety. You're miles from anyone else, there's no real danger, and nothing to be afraid of. I often took a forest siesta before starting back to work, just closing my eyes and letting go for a while. So refreshing!

Now I live in Spain, far from the rain and the damp of the dewy Irish woodlands. I miss it sometimes, but all is not lost. Although forestry in the southeast of Spain is not nearly as widespread as it is back in Ireland, and the trees tend to stick closer to the ground, I've still found one or two favorite spots where I can slowly walk and think. If you have watched any of my videos on AlcoholMastery.com, you will have seen me trundling through the peaks and valleys of one of my favorite forests, just outside Guardamar, where I used to live. These Valencian forests offer much of that same magic that I found back in the West of Ireland. All the sounds and scents of nature are still there, the overall atmosphere, none of that changes. The heat and dryness create a different baseline, the bird song is maybe a little different, and then there's the cicadas. These jumping insects used to get so loud they threatened to drown out what I was saying on some of the videos. I think no matter where I go in the world, I'm always going to be looking for that unique forest environment, seeking out that special tranquility and temporary solitude.

What to Do

1. When you practice Shinrin-Yoku, the idea is to soak up as much of the atmosphere as you can, so don't rush. If you are walking, walk at a slow pace, no more than a mile an hour - a little over a kilometer. Take time to sit and rest every so often

2. You don't even have to walk, you can just sit and enjoy, it's up to you. .

3. Forest bathing is another form of meditation, but you don't need to treat it like meditation. There's no requirement to be quiet. It's about just breathing in that unique atmosphere. Read a book, think, contemplate, or just be in the moment. Let the forest do its job.

4. What's the best time to forest bathe? Anytime you want. It depends on you. What's your favorite time of the year? That's a good time to forest bathe. Some people prefer autumn, which offers its own blend of magnificent colors and smells. Other people prefer spring when everything is just beginning to pop. I love the summer, the heat and dryness. I love listening to nature get on with its life.

5. Don't stray too far. Taking a drive to your local forest is something everyone should do at least a couple of times a month. But you have to be careful. The sheer size of some forests make getting lost a real possibility. So, be sure you know the area well before venturing inside too far. Stick to the paths as much as possible.

6. Many forests are designed for public access, with safety in mind. Other forests, although still open to the public, might be working forests which are not so well taken care of.

7. Take note of the weather forecast before you leave home and take appropriate clothing with you. The forest in the rain will be a lot different than on a warm summer's day. It can be just as enjoyable, if not more so. You just need to be prepared. There's nothing relaxing about being soaked and cold. Everything can be very slippery after a rain shower, so be sure to bring appropriate footwear.

8. Don't go near a forest in high winds. There is a real possibility of trees or branches falling.

9. Don't go forest bathing too late in the evening. Getting lost in the dark might mean spending the night. The forest at night is a whole different prospect.

10. Always carry a first aid kit.

11. Consider taking a pal, especially if you have problems with mobility.

49. Everyone Shines Given the Right Lighting

"All the darkness in the world cannot extinguish the light of a single candle."

Francis of Assisi

Our perceptions can be altered instantly through the colors in our environment. A warm sunny day feels a lot different than an overcast and gray day. So if you want to instantly alter the mood of your environment, change the lighting.

Dr. George Brainard, who has directed the Light Research Program at Thomas Jefferson University since 1984 says, "Controlled experiments have shown that light at the right intensity and wavelength can have alerting effects and that dimmer, long-wavelength light can help prepare for sleep."

For instance, green lighting can help to reduce tension, nervousness, anxiety, and depression. As we saw in the last section, one of the most relaxing places on the planet is in the middle of a forest, surrounded by green.

Dim red lights work really well as night lights. They are the least likely to disrupt your sleep or rouse you too much. If you often need to use the loo during the night, put a soft, low-watt red bulb in your bathroom. You won't wake you up as much as a normal light bulb.

What to Do

1. The simplest way of changing the ambiance of a room is by changing the bulbs for colored ones, which you can find in most

hardware stores.

2. You can also buy some high heat resistant spray paint from your local DIY store and paint ordinary white bulbs to whatever color you choose.

3. If you use low heat CFLs or LEDs, you can drape a piece of light colored material over a lampshade. Don't allow the material to come directly in contact with the bulb - just to be on the safe side.

50. Two Acorns and a Hammock

"An optimist is a man who plants two acorns and buys a hammock"

Jean de Lattre de Tassigny

A hammock is a swinging bed made of netting or some other material. We've all seen the halcyon image of a hammock tied between two palm trees on a beach with the sun in the background. It's one of the most iconic images associated with relaxation and the care-free life.

Using a hammock to wind-down, even for a few minutes every day, can dramatically reduce your stress levels. There's just something particularly special about the way a hammock clings to your body, especially the wide Mexican style hammock, and gently rocks you to and fro. I imagine it has something to do with mentally transporting you back to the secure feeling of infancy, swaddled in warm blankets and softly swayed in the arms of your mother.

What to Do

1. If you have a couple of trees in your back garden, close enough to hang a hammock, tie the hammock between them and you're good to go.

2. You can buy a hammock that comes with its own stand for about $100 on Amazon or eBay.

3. If you only have a small space available, not enough for a stand, you can use hooks between two walls. Once you have finished with the hammock, you just unhook it and store it away

ready for your next relaxation appointment. Take a look on YouTube for some tips on how to hang your hammock.

51. Learning to Handle Discomfort - Cold Shower Therapy

We've all heard the benefits of having a cold shower if you're a little on the excited side, if you know what I mean! A cold shower also works if you're feeling stressed. Try it! You'll be amazed at how much energy you can draw from that cold water splashing all over your skin. Once you get over the initial shock that is!

The science is pretty straightforward. When your body comes into contact with cold water, the blood vessels just under the surface of your skin contract, moving the blood away from the surface and towards your core. Your body does this to protect your core temperature which operates within a very narrow band to keep the body's normal enzymatic reactions stable. As your blood moves inward, away from your skin, it bathes the interior of your body, including your brain, with fresh blood. This brings an influx of nutrients and oxygen with it. As your body reheats, the blood moves back towards the surface, carrying away some of the toxins that had accumulated at your core.

Another way of using cold showers is to acclimate yourself to being in discomfort. If you are about to quit drinking and you fear the discomfort you might go through, try taking a cold shower for 30 days. As you stand in the shower, getting ready to turn that tap onto the cold setting, every fiber of your body will be screaming at you, telling you what an idiot you are. Who does this kind of perverted thing? Are you crazy? Why would you want to do this?

Don't worry about the discomfort, it's nothing really. Stepping into a shower for five minutes, while cold water splashes on your body, involves very small consequences. You will feel a bit more refreshed but not much else. The only person who's affected is you, no one else. If you can't stand this discomfort, ask yourself how long you're going to last when you are faced with discomfort in a situation where the consequences are much more life altering for you and the people that you love?

What to Do

1. First, get over the psychological hurdle of actually doing it. The cold that you think about in your mind as you imagine taking a cold shower is much worse than the cold actually is. It's only cold water!

2. Turn on the shower to the coldest setting and wait for a good stream to pour forth.

3. Step under the shower and do what you would normally do.

4. Stay in the shower for as long as you can... 5 minutes is a good target.

5. Get out and towel off...

How good does that feel!

This is not going to harm you if you have a normal healthy heart and blood pressure. If in doubt, ask your doctor.

52. Buzz Your Mind with New Adventures

"A mind that is stretched by a new experience can never go back to its old dimensions"

Oliver Wendell Holmes

Variety is the spice of life. Much of the time when I'm feeling down in the dumps, anxious, or depressed, I'm just bored. It's easy to mistake boredom for depression. I normally feel this way after I've gone through a few weeks working on the same project, doing the same thing day in and day out, and following the same timetable. Once I examine the feelings and think about the underlying causes, it's easy to see what's happening and where the problem lies, I'm simply bored. I'm not getting any new stimulation from my life.

Usually I can fix this with a walk, my favorite reconditioner. Sometimes it takes a bit more effort, doing something I haven't done for a while or something I've never done before, a new adventure.

Worrying and thinking about all the things that are wrong with you or your life is a recipe for anxiety and depression. I've already talked about motion changing emotion. This is the process where you can change how you think and feel by changing your physiology and your surroundings. If you're at home, feeling anxious about quitting, why allow yourself to linger in that mood, get up and do something. Do some exercises, dance, do the dishes, clean your house, blow up some balloons, anything.

If that doesn't work, you probably need a change of scenery. As I said earlier, just getting out of the house for a walk is normally all it takes to lift my spirits. You'll find the same thing. Once you change your scene, your mood and thoughts are likely to follow. When you can change what you see you can change what you think. Of course this won't work every time, sometimes you're going to need to venture a little further afield, to do something a little more out of the ordinary.

What to Do

1. Go somewhere you've never been before. Where should you go? It depends on where you live, the time of year, and the time of day or night. Seek out something you've never done before, a place or a situation you've never been. Challenge your beliefs about what you're capable of doing.

2. How about going to a museum or an art gallery, a church, mosque, or synagogue. Try a new restaurant. Go to the movies. Buy tickets for a movie you would never ordinarily think about seeing. Buy a book you wouldn't normally read. Visit the library. Start a conversation with a stranger. Just sit in familiar location and try to see things from a different angle, look for things that you've never seen before. Sign up to learn a new skill. Go foraging in your local woodlands.

3. There is an endless supply of new things to do, especially if you can look at some of your routine activities in a new light. For instance, there's a couple of walks that I really like to take, close to where I live. These dirt tracks bring me over a local pine-covered hill overlooking the Mediterranean. The path then comes down along some old dry riverbeds, through orange and lemon groves, and back to where my moped is parked. You've probably seen a lot of that walk in some of my videos. If I get fed up doing the same route, I just reverse it and everything looks fresh.

4. Make a list of the places, things, situations, and people that can bring some novelty and creativity into your life. When you feel anxious or bored, take out your list and do one of the items. Aim to cross each item from your list. Then start a new list.

53. Puzzling Out Your Ravenous Brain

Have you ever become so engrossed in playing a game or a figuring out a puzzle that time just seemed to fly by? This is another form of getting into the zone that Mihaly Csikszentmihalyi talks about in his book, Flow. He calls it completely focused motivation. In the main, playing games and fiddling over puzzles can be seen as interruption, diverting you away from the things you should be doing. Then there are other times, when distraction is healthy. Mental puzzles can be a healthy distraction in your life, helping you to reboot your thoughts, and to fight off the worries that might never happen. Puzzling through a crossword, fighting your way through a flock of cartoon angry birds, or patiently flipping through a game of solitaire could be just the thing you need.

Here are some reasons why puzzles and games are good for you:

1. They concentrate your mind and move it away from worry. Like a camera lens, you can only focus on one thing at a time.

2. Because you know there's a solution, decoding a puzzle or working your way through a game teaches you the art of patience and determination.

3. Solving puzzles is another form of meditation. Remember, the basis for all mediation is focusing your mind on the present moment.

4. Figuring out solutions allows you to develop your thinking

skills across many facets.

5. Working out one part of your brain allows the rest of your brain take a break.

6. Distracting your brain with an intricate puzzle pulls your attention away from your body, allowing it to relax.

7. Puzzles and game play make a healthy alternative form of instant gratification.

8. They're inexpensive.

In the first few days and weeks of your new journey away from alcohol, you can use puzzles and games as trigger diverters, diverting your mind away from the alcohol thoughts or triggers.

Daniel Bor, a neuroscientist with the University of Sussex in the UK, explains why some people spend hours struggling over a puzzle in his book, *The Ravenous Brain: How the New Science of Consciousness Explains Our Insatiable Search for Meaning*. He asks "Why do we love crossword puzzles and why are people addicted to Sudoku? That's what a huge bit of the cortex is primed to do — to spot [patterns] — and once we spot them we can assimilate them into our pyramid of knowledge and build more layers of strategy, and knowing how to do that makes us incredibly successful at controlling the world."

What to Do

1. Play indoor puzzles or games on your own. Relax in a comfortable chair while you work your way through a crossword puzzle, Sudoku, or word search. Throw darts at a dart board. Download some solo games like solitaire, minesweeper, or angry birds. You'll find free online versions of these and many others for your phone, tablet, or computer. Have a crack at your kid's game console.

2. Playing indoor games with others adds the benefits of social interaction and support. As in the previous example, use the modern technology at your fingertips. Most electronic games have multi-player functionality. Or you can go back to the more traditional games like chess, draughts, Monopoly, or Trivial

Pursuit. If you're feeling adventurous, try a game of twister.

3. Outdoor games tend to be a bit more physical, so you get the best of both worlds. Games like golf, tennis, or football, require the same levels of focus and concentration as do their indoor counterparts and they throw a good workout into the bargain.

54. Explore Deep Inside and Discover What Your True Voice is Shouting

"I never travel without my diary. One should always have something sensational to read on the train".

Oscar Wilde

Journaling or expressive writing can be cathartic and constructive. Have you ever had the feeling that your mind is running around in circles, like a broken record, skipping back and forward with no apparent direction? Pulling the thoughts out of your head and setting them out on paper allows you to focus on what's really worrying you. Stress can come about through confusion over what's really happening in our lives. When we're in this anxious state, our thoughts tend to be fuzzy, scattered, and unfocused. Writing your thoughts down on paper gives you clarity. It lets you unscramble the mess.

Writing your thoughts helps to highlight your underlying concerns and issues, giving you a window into what's really going on.

Flannery O'Connor said, "I write because I don't know what I think until I read what I say."

As you fill out the page in front of you, your sentences will often reveal that you're stressing-out for no valid reason. Unfettered worries left spinning around in a confused mind often lead to fear. By organizing your worried thoughts through the writing process, you soon realize that there's no substance behind most of your fears. In the words of FDR, "The only thing we have to fear is fear itself".

Writing in a focused manner, for at least five or ten minutes a day, is another form of meditation. Journaling laser targets your energies onto the thoughts behind the stress and away from the feelings of stress. As you progress with this form of self-therapy, you'll find yourself writing for longer periods of time, unplugging from your daily routine and recharging your batteries.

What to Do

There are a number of methods of writing that you can implement. I'm going to talk about two here, journaling and garbage writing.

Journaling

1. Start by sorting out which writing medium you are going to use. Some people are comfortable using their computer or tablet, others find that using a pen and paper can be more grounding and therapeutic. Each medium has its advantages and disadvantages. I prefer the old-fashioned method. Taking out a pad and pen lets me turn off everything else. With no distractions or noise from my computer, my thoughts flow a lot easier, I can hear myself think. Writing in this medium lets me my diary with me when I go out. I put it into my backpack and head off for a hike in the mountains or along the beach. I don't have to think about finding a power point or batteries running out. When I think of something to say, I can pull out my notebook and write it down. If I don't, I'll most likely forget it by the time I get home. So my journal also acts as a backup memory.

2. Set aside some time and find a place where you won't be disturbed.

3. Put the date at the top of the page and just start writing.

4. Write in a stream of consciousness. This means just putting the thoughts onto the paper as they come into your head. Don't concern yourself too much with grammar or spelling, sentence structure or paragraphs, just write. This is the time where you can turn off the filter between your mind and the pen. Just write as it

comes out.

5. You're the only person that will see this so don't worry about being judged and never judge yourself. This is not a writing competition.

6. The idea is to write for a set amount of time. Start off with five minutes and work your way to ten or twenty minutes.

7. Stream of consciousness writing means you need to continue to write even if you can't think of what to say. Write something like "I can't think of what to say, I can't think of what to say". Or just write the same word over and over. Your brain will eventually throw out something logical into your writing. If you find yourself going off topic, gently bring your mind back to the problem.

Garbage writing

1. Garbage writing means writing your worries or stresses onto a piece of paper.

2. Instead of journaling, where the intention is to keep your work, garbage writing is meant as a form of catharsis.

3. Take a single loose piece of paper and pen.

4. You don't have to add the date, just start writing in the stream of consciousness style as outlined above.

5. Write everything that is troubling you about yourself, your journey ahead, your past, whatever.

6. Write the nasty things that your Gollum voice is bitching on to you, things like "You're not good enough", "I can't do this", or "I really need a drink".

7. When you are finished, physically scrunch up the paper and throw it into the garbage. That's it!

A study in Spain, involving Spanish high school students showed this to be an excellent method of clearing your mind of those unwanted roundabout thoughts that keep spinning about in your mind. The students who went through the process of garbage writing reported that they had fewer negative thoughts about themselves, their body image, and their overall self-image. One of the researchers behind the study, Richard Petty said, "Of course, even if you throw the thoughts in a garbage can or put them in the recycle bin on the computer, they are not really gone -- you can regenerate them. But the representations of those thoughts are gone, at least temporarily, and it seems to make it easier to not think about them."

55. Creating Your Arsenal of Positivity Weapons

Like journaling, creating your own positivity list is an alternative method of sorting through the jumble in your mind. Making a list focuses your thought onto the good things in your life. When you focus on positive thoughts, it is very difficult to remain in a negative frame of mind, and that includes feeling depressed. Socrates said that, "The secret of change is to focus all of your energy, not on fighting the old, but on building the new." Look forwards and the adventure begins.

What to Do

1. Take a sheet of paper or open up a blank document on your computer or laptop.

2. Write a numbered list and try to get to at least 100.

3. Make each item on your list about the things in your life that are making you happy or have made you feel happy in the past. Your can list your achievements to date, writing down all the things you have overcome in your life. Some other ideas include the hobbies or other interests you have developed, the sports you play, the positives about your health (I've got great teeth, a healthy heart, a functioning liver, and so on), the positives about your family, friends, or home.

My list concentrates on my personal achievements. I take out my list and go over it when I'm feeling like I can't push past a certain barrier in my life. It helps me to overcome self-doubt when my mind is doubting my abilities to accomplish the things that I've set out for myself.

My list contains over 500 achievements that I've made in my life. I soon as I achieve something new, I write it down. My list even includes such early achievements as learning how to walk and talk, to tie my shoelaces, and learning how to read. These accomplishments may seem very simple, but when I was learning how to do them, as it is for all of us, they weren't simple at all, they were very difficult. But we all triumph in the end. We learn those massive skills of walking and running and talking and thinking. I listen to my nieces who can speak two languages fluently. They can flip back and forth between English and Spanish with such ease and composure, depending on who they are speaking to.

Also on my list, I've written my achievements like learning how to make a whacking curry, to fix my Land Rover engine, and to grow my own garlic.

I keep this list as a part of my 'smile file', which I'll be talking about in a later section.

When I'm feeling down on myself, I take out this list and see all the achievements I've already completed, and each one is a personal success story. That's the big takeout here. Each of your personal success stories proves that yes, you can do it! Yes, you are a competent, intelligent, efficient, and talented person! Yes, your life is filled with accomplishment!

Recently, I was feeling pessimistic about my abilities to learn Spanish. I got out my list and came across the item saying that I had learned how to write and speak in English. Having already successfully learned to speak and write in a language proves that I can do it, I've already done it once, so there's absolutely no reason that I can't do it again.

56. Up, Up, and Away

Here's another few balloon themed stress busters for you to try.

There's something about balloons that just capture the imagination. Have you ever let go of a helium balloon outside and watched it drift away into the clouds until you couldn't see it any more, wondering where it would end up?

Hot air ballooning is on my bucket list of things to do. I like the idea of floating in absolute peace and quiet with a bird's eye view over the world.

If you want to take to the skies, there are many places throughout the world where you can hire the services of a hot air balloon for very reasonable prices. But it's not something most people can do at the drop of a hat just because you're feeling a little tense. However, there are more down-to-earth types of ballooning which are more affordable and can be done immediately.

I've already covered blowing up balloons for relaxation in a previous section. Here, I'm going to cover three more types of ballooning, balloon breathing, balloon visualization, and ballooning off your worries.

What to Do

1. Balloon Breathing

Balloon breathing does not actually require a balloon. It is a very simple relaxation technique which involves breathing primarily using your stomach muscles. With this yoga technique, you inhale long deep breathes using your diaphragm. As you breathe in, let your stomach expand outward as much as possible, then allow your chest to expand fully, pulling air into your lungs until they are full. Hold at the top for 3 or 4 seconds before breathing out, letting your chest deflate first and then your belly.

This breathing technique quickly fills your blood with oxygen.

2. Balloon Visualizations

Sit in a comfortable chair. Take a couple of deep breathes and close your eyes. Relax your body and listen to the sound of your breathing as you slowly inhale and exhale.

Take a couple of minutes to drift, letting each part of your body relax. Start at your toes and feet, move up your legs, relaxing all the muscles on the way. Relax your torso, then your arms and hands. Relax your neck and head muscles.

When you are fully relaxed, visualize yourself sitting in a meadow, surrounded by green grass. You can feel the early summer sun warming your face. In front of you is a huge hot air balloon with a wicker basket hanging underneath, floating just above the grass. Now visualize pulling all your worries out of yourself and placing them one by one into the basket. When you have no more worries left inside, when all your worries have been placed into the basket, release the tethers from the balloon and watch as it floats gently into the sky. As it rises into the sky, the air currents carrying the balloon into the distance, your worries are carried further and further away until eventually the balloon becomes no more than a pinprick and finally disappears from view.

Continue to relax, noticing how light you feel now that you've been relieved of all your worries. Slowly open your eyes. Carry the relaxation feelings with you throughout your day.

3. Ballooning off Your Worries

This technique is very similar to balloon visualizations except you do it for real. Instead of using a hot air balloon, you need a helium filled balloon, some string, a piece of paper, a pen or marker, and you'll be using the garbage writing from a couple of sections ago.

Using a stream of consciousness form of writing, put all your worries onto a piece of paper, front and back (use more than one sheet if you need to).

Roll up the paper into a small tube and attach it to your helium balloon with a piece of string or some sticky tape.

Alternatively, you can use a marker to write a few words onto the balloon itself.

Take the balloon outside. If you can find a tranquil spot away from people, all the better.

Let your balloon go and watch as your worries slowly drift away into the distance.

Again, these techniques only get rid of the representations of your worries, not the worries themselves. It does seem to make it easier not to think about them though. This is particularly helpful if your worries are groundless, if they pertain to issues of self-belief or self-confidence for instance.

57. The Ultimate Relaxation

Reading is one of my life passions. Given the opportunity, I would read for most of the day, at least until my eyes started to spin. Reading is something I try to fit in every morning and it's the last thing I do before I nod off to sleep at night.

Reading is one of the most relaxing things you can do. Again, it goes back to the mind focusing on one thing, blocking the outside world in favor of your inside world, another form of meditation, putting yourself into the state of flow.

Researchers at the University of Sussex in the UK conducted some stress tests in 2009. The idea was to elevate the heart rate and levels of stress in the participants using a range of activities. Then the volunteers were put through some relaxation techniques. Reading came out on top.

The lead researcher in the experiment, Dr. David Lewis said, "Losing yourself in a book is the ultimate relaxation". Surprisingly, they didn't have to read for long before noticing a response. In most cases, they only had to read for 6 minutes before their relaxation levels were lowered. Dr. Lewis went on to say, "This is more than merely a distraction but an active engaging of the imagination as the words on the printed page stimulate your creativity and cause you to enter what is essentially an altered state of consciousness".

What to Do

1. Find a good book to read.

Dr. Lewis had this to say about what book you should read, "It really doesn't matter what book you read, by losing yourself in a thoroughly engrossing book you can escape from the worries and stresses of the everyday world and spend a while exploring the domain of the author's imagination." For me, the main thing is to choose a book where the topic or plot has piqued your interest.

2. Choose a topic which is going to relax you. News type topics should be avoided.

3. Choose a topic that has personal interest to you. Self-help books are great for spurring you on but they might not be the best material for relaxation. Find a novel where you can disappear into another world. I always read self-help, biography, psychology, and so on during the day. At night, when I want to relax, I read novels, mostly sci-fi and fantasy.

4. Set aside some time, say 30 minutes, when you know you're not going to be disturbed.

5. Find a place where you know you're not going to be disturbed.

6. Get comfortable and start reading.

Should you read a proper book or with a device? It's up to you. Whatever you feel the most comfortable with. I read both. At night I only read on my iPhone. I can turn the back-light way down so I'm not disturbed by the screen glow. I read until I can't keep my eyes open. I've only dropped the phone a couple of times, but it's well protected. My phone fits nicely in my hand and I can turn the pages easily using my thumb. I can also alter the text size, which is a factor now I'm getting older. I want to avoid wearing my glasses to be for as long as possible.

58. The Most Beautiful Fraud in the World

Just as reading a great book can take you away from the pressures of life, so can watching a great movie. I haven't been to the cinema in a while, but it's still a place that I find magical. The plush seats, the giant screen and equally big sound, filing into your seat, popcorn and drink in hand, waiting for the lights to dim and the curtain the pull back is just exciting. Sociologist and film theorist Siegfried Kracauer says, "In the theater, I am always I. But in the cinema, I dissolve into all things and beings." And Jean-Luc Godard said, "Cinema is the most beautiful fraud in the world." I couldn't agree more!

Let's face it, the cost of going to the movies can add up quickly, especially if you're taking the whole family. Once you factor in the cost of getting there, the tickets, food and drinks, it can stack up to quite a bit of money. It's super easy to recreate many of the best elements of a good night at the movies in your own home. Large screen TVs are not too expensive and are getting cheaper all the time. It's very simple to whip up some popcorn and drinks. Remember, this is all about relaxation and stress relief, so try to avoid the sugary stuff if you can. If you can't, enjoy anyway!

What to Do

1. Choose your movie. Go to your local store or download from Amazon or Netflix. Here's a list of some of my favorite feel-good movies.

Big - Tom Hanks

Finding Forrester - Sean Connery

It's a Wonderful Life - James Stewart

Casablanca - Humphrey Bogart, Ingrid Bergman

Eternal Sunshine of a Spotless Mind - Jim Carey, Kate Winslett

Little Miss Sunshine - Greg Kinnear, Steve Carell, Abigail Breslin

The Blues Brothers - John Belushi, Dan Ackroyd

Trading Places - Eddie Murphy, Dan Ackroyd

Groundhog Day - Bill Murray

Moulin Rouge - Ewan McGregor, Nicole Kidman

2. Gather together your movie treats.

3. Set the ambiance with low lights and comfy seats.

4. If you're watching an all-time favorite, get into character. Dress up like one of the characters in the movie.

5. Enjoy!

59. Instant Gratification Quote Therapy

Here's just a short list of some quotes that bring me inspiration or motivation. It's instant gratification quote therapy.

What to Do

Keep a list of quotes on hand for when you need a boost in motivation or confidence. Put them into your arsenal of positivity. Write them on sticky notes or A4 sheets of paper and post them around your home. The quote above my desk now says "This moment is the only moment where you can do anything." I don't know where it comes from.

The ones below are just a selection of mine. Use them or find your own, there are millions of magnificent quotes on the internet, a click or two away.

"By believing passionately in that which doesn't exist, you create it and that which has not been sufficiently desired is what we call the non-existent."

Nikos Kazantzakis

"Each morning when I open my eyes I say to myself: I, not events, have the power to make me happy or unhappy today. I can choose which it shall be. Yesterday is dead, tomorrow hasn't arrived yet. I have just one day, today, and I'm going to be happy in it."

Groucho Marks

"It isn't what you have, or who you are, or where you are, or what you are doing that makes you happy or unhappy. It is what you think about."

Dale Carnegie

"Faith is taking the first step even when you can't see the whole staircase."

Martin Luther King Jr.

"You are not useless. You are not hopeless. And no matter how scared you are, you will never be alone. And deep down, somewhere, in the part of you that decided the good days and your happiness and your health were all worth fighting for, you know that, too. Hold onto that knowledge. It will see you through the worst."

Ella Ceron

"The pain that you've been feeling, can't compare to the joy that's coming."

Romans 8:18

"Keep your thoughts positive because your thoughts become your words. Keep your words positive because your words become your behavior. Keep your behavior positive because your behavior becomes your habits. Keep your habits positive because your habits become your values. Keep your values positive because your values become your destiny."

Mahatma Ghandi

"Don't wish it was easier, wish you were better. Don't wish for less problems, wish for more skills. Don't wish for less challenges, wish for more wisdom. The major value in life is not what you get. The major value in life is what you become. Success is not to be pursued; it is to be attracted by the person you become."

Jim Rohn

"For every minute you are angry you lose sixty seconds of happiness."

Ralph Waldo Emerson

"Folks are usually about as happy as they make their minds up to be."

Abraham Lincoln

"I've got nothing to do today but smile."

Paul Simon

"If we're growing, we're always going to be out of our comfort zone."

John Maxwell

"If you wait to do everything until you're sure it's right, you'll probably never do much of anything."

Win Borden

"Shoot for the moon. Even if you miss, you'll land among the stars."

Brian Littrell

"People often say that motivation doesn't last. Well, neither does bathing – that's why we recommend it daily."

Zig Ziglar

"Motivation is what gets you started. Habit is what keeps you going."

Jim Rohn

"When it is obvious that the goals cannot be reached, don't adjust the goals, adjust the action steps."

Confucius

"All that we are is the result of what we have thought."

Buddha

"We are what we repeatedly do. Excellence, then, is not an act, but a habit."

Aristotle

"Notice that the stiffest tree is most easily cracked, while the bamboo or willow survives by bending with the wind."

Bruce Lee

60. Patience is the Gold of Time - Growing a Bonsai

If you are looking for a way to relax, do something pleasant, and express some of your more artful instincts, think about growing a bonsai tree. The art of the bonsai is not really in the growing, nature takes care of that part, it's about the tending for the grower and the contemplation for the onlooker. You can be both, tender one minute and onlooker the next.

This tending involves pruning, shaping, and training your bonsai so that it can live. Bonsai means plantings in a tray and is often used in English to denote any miniature tree grown in a pot or container.

Master bonsai cultivator and teacher, John Yoshio Naka says, "Bonsai is not the result: that comes after. Your enjoyment is what is important". He speaks about the bonsai having "philosophy, botany, artistry, human quality behind it…" He explains the art form by saying, "The bonsai is not you working on the tree; you have to have the tree work on you." That's my attraction. Growing a bonsai is something a little bit special, something you have to put your heart and soul into.

You don't need green fingers or much experience to take care of a bonsai tree, but you do need dedication. In the botanical world, bonsais are one of the more challenging plants to grow. I think this is the beauty of the challenge, a simple need to nurture and care for the plant or it's going to die. There are many rewards to be found in taking care of this little piece of living art. Apart from the relaxation that any dedicated past-time will bring you,

you'll also find a great satisfaction in knowing that you have mastered a craft.

Let's take a look at how you can get started in the bonsai world and a few tips on keeping your tree alive and thriving.

What to Do

1. Get yourself a basic book on the subject. If you would like to give it a go, there are plenty of books on Amazon which will give you a much more detailed description of what to do and what to avoid. Here, I want to give you a quick rundown of the basics, just to give you a feel for it.

2. Pruning your Bonsai

Bonsai pruning can be seen as a miniature version of topiary, which is the art of clipping bushes and hedges into fanciful or ornate shapes. When pruning a bonsai, you first decide on the direction you'd like the branches to grow and the form you would like your bonsai to take. You should use specialist pruning scissors and bonsai specific wire to achieve the shape that you want. You can prune the greenery during the growing cycle but leave the woody pruning for the dormant cycle.

3. Placing your Bonsai

Your bonsai should spend most of its life in the great outdoors. Don't keep it indoors for more than 7 days at time. This won't do your plant any good. A good outdoor location is out of the direct sunlight. You can move your plant around during the day to keep it in the shade. Otherwise, find a spot where it's going to be in the shade most of the day. The best way of knowing if your plant is getting too much or too little light is by observation. If the bonsai starts to wilt, move it to a spot that isn't getting as much light.

4. Watering your Bonsai?

There is no set rule to how much water a bonsai's needs. It depends on many factors like the time of year or the temperature. The best rule of thumb is to check the soil. Poke around and see if the soil needs water. If it's damp, don't water. If it's dry, water it. During the winter months, you'll hardly need to water at all. If you live in a climate with rain at least once or twice a week, that should be plenty.

61. A Different Vision of Life - Learning a New Language

When you learn to speak a new language, you improve the performance of your brain in three key areas, communication, recognition, and understanding. Learning can overcome boredom, spark your brain into life, and involve you in a new culture. You also learn how to multitask. Multitasking is not about doing two or more things at once, it's about the speed at which you can switch between the two things. Building your abilities to switch between two languages will translate to other areas of your life.

Learning to speak a new language will improve your memory. Your brain is your most important tool, to keep it sharp you must use it. Alcohol affects both your long-term and short-term memory. It is one of the few substances that can get through your blood brain barrier and directly affect the electrical and chemical processes in your head. Whether you're trying to improve your memory after quitting drinking or just improve your memory overall, learning a second language is one of the best ways of doing this. Because you need to learn new words, associations, and structures, you improve and remap vital areas in your brain. Learning a new language will also help you to become a better perceiver, your decision making skills will improve, and your grasp of your own language will improve as you learn the mechanics of the new language.

What to Do

1. First choose the language you want to learn. Be sure to choose a language that you are likely to use. Don't just learn a

language because you like the way it sounds. This can be a bonus, but it shouldn't be your primary motivation. A language is a method of communication, first and foremost. If you can't communicate in the language, what's the point! Do you have a large Spanish community near you who you can practice with? Do you like visiting a particular country where your language would come in handy?

2. Get some proper training. There are many free online resources where you can get your feet wet. The only problem with free courses is that tend not to be very structured. As a beginner in any new language, you're better off purchasing a basic language learning course, one that will take you to at least intermediate level. There are plenty to choose from including Linguaphone, Pimsleur, and Michel Thomas. You can also hire natural speakers through websites such as italki.com for very little money. For instance, I have regular Spanish conversations with my teacher in Madrid via Skype and she only charges $10 an hour.

3. Don't get too caught up in learning direct translations. One of the biggest mistakes I made when learning to speak my passable Spanish was trying to directly translate my sentences from English to Spanish. This works well for short sentences. But most of the time you'll end up sounding stilted and becoming frustrated with your efforts. Begin by learning some of the phrases you'd need to know if you were having a friendly conversation with a normal person, or those you'll need when taking a vacation, going shopping, or ordering in a restaurant. To repeat, learning a new language is all about communication. Think about where you will be likely to use your new language skills and learn for those situations.

62. Swear Like a Pirate

Mark Twain said, "When angry, count to four. When very angry, swear."

Did you ever use foul language as an automatic response to stubbing your toe or knocking your shin off the living room table? According to research carried out by Richard Stephens of Keele University in the UK, swearing is closely related to being emotionally aroused.

Dr. Stephens says, "Swearing has been around for centuries and is an almost universal human linguistic phenomenon. It taps into emotional brain centres and appears to arise in the right brain, whereas most language production occurs in the left cerebral hemisphere of the brain. Our research shows one potential reason why swearing developed and why it persists."

In his book, The Stuff of Thought, Steven Pinker of Harvard compares swearing to the reactions of a cat that has just been sat on. He writes, "I suspect that swearing taps into a defensive reflex in which an animal that is suddenly injured or confined erupts in a furious struggle, accompanied by an angry vocalization, to startle and intimidate an attacker."

Not only does swearing ease the pain of an accidental hammer blow to the thumb, according to one psychologist who has studied foul language use for more than three decades, "It allows us to vent or express anger, joy, surprise, happiness." Timothy Jay of Massachusetts College of Liberal Arts goes on to say, "It's like the horn on your car, you can do a lot of things with that, it's built into you."

In Germany, if you want to let off a bit of steam, you can call a hotline called "Swear Away" where you can curse at a stranger to your heart's content. "Swear Away" or "Schimpf-los" in German, is manned 24/7 by operators whose only job is to take your abuse. If you find yourself at a loss for words, your paid call companion will prompt you with a little provocation of their own. Maybe this is a bargain at the €1.49 per minute price tag. It could certainly save you getting into a lot of trouble if you set off your outburst at the wrong person.

What to Do

1. We all know how to swear, it's one of the most automatic reactions. The level of swearing you personally use depends on you as a person, but we all do it. In Ireland, it's considered bad form to use the name of Jesus in vain, so many people will say Jaysus, but with every bit as much ferocity as the real thing. They also say feck instead of fuck. So you don't have to actually swear if you don't want to, use your own version. When I want to swear I use the real thing and lots of it.

2. Swearing at someone else might relieve a lot of stress for you, but it might get you in trouble. So try to avoid aiming your swearing at other people.

3. Regardless of which version of swearing you use, the full-force pirate swearing or the censored version, take yourself off to a quiet spot by yourself and swear until you feel better.

63. Wacky Works and Smile File

For me, iPod playlists are an absolute godsend. I bought my iPod about 10 years ago, which holds 160 GB of music. Even though I've never filled it up, it's about half full as I write, 80 GB is a lot of music to have floating around on any one device. The playlist function allows me to group songs or albums together in one place. I have a playlist for relaxation, another for music I listen to while I write. I have a playlist for meditation, for language learning, and a playlist for exercise. One of my most used playlists is what I call my Wacky Works. I use this playlist when I need to lift my spirits. It contains all my feel-good music, as well as a lot of old comedy sketches, like Monty Python, Derek and Clive, and so on.

This Wacky Works concept can be applied to other areas of your life. It doesn't have to be an iTunes playlist. It can be a simple shoe box with all the things that make you smile. Photographs that spark fabulous memories, instantly brightening up your day. Books or movies that inspire you to get up and create the life you want to live, music that lifts your spirits and makes you want to dance, stories you've cut out of magazines that put a smile on your face, or images of the things you would like to have in your life, a better home, a car, or a dream vacation. I have a plastic box that I bought from the local Chinese store with stories, magazine pictures, old photos, birthday cards, letters, and so on. I call it my Smile File.

We all get those days when we feel a bit off-color. It's just a part of life. There's nothing wrong with it per se, but I think we have a choice of wallowing in the self-pity of our 'bad' day, or choosing to do something about it. For the most part, there's never anyone else affected by your moods except you, so why not choose to be in a good mood. Your smile file is your personal mood altering Aladdin's cave. You don't need drugs to pick you up, you never did. There are already plenty of wonderful things in your life to do that for you. A Smile File or Wacky Works is just a simple way of reminding yourself about all those great things. Play some of your most uplifting music as you root through your Smile File.

My Smile Files and Wacky Works never fail to cheer me up, to take my mind away from my worries, and to help me to see the good things in my life.

What to Do

1. Your Wacky Works is your go-to place for cheering yourself up. All the items should be very personal and dear to you, don't include anything that makes you feel sad.

2. Find a large box, a fancy chest, or whatever feels right to you. It could be just a simple folder on your desktop with your movies, music, images, notes, poems, and so on. I have both, a computer folder with music, movies, sketches, etc, and a plastic container with a lid.

3. How do you decide what goes into the Wacky Works or Smile File? Only put things into your Works that give you a nice feeling when you interact with them. How many items? It's another personal choice, but don't overdo it or you'll just get overwhelmed. If you are dedicating a file on your computer to this, you have a lot more leeway for organization, using sub-files to separate your stuff according to type.

4. Enhance the lift you get by creating the right environment. Sit in a comfortable chair, light a candle or two, light a joss stick, put on some energizing music.

64. Tell Your Worries to Get Lost

Worrying is a complete waste of your time, energy, and sanity. The word 'worry' comes from the Old English 'wrygan', meaning *to strangle.* In the 17th century, people used the word to mean *to bother, distress, or persecute.* That's about what we do to ourselves with our worry, we bother, distress, or persecute ourselves, and we do it over what? Things that might never happen, for the most part!

When our ancestors lived in the caves, worrying was a natural part of their lives. Worrying was a survival mechanism that kept them in one piece, focusing their minds on staying out of danger. When you're one of the hunted, worrying makes sense. It creates over-cautiousness that can save your life. Unfortunately, our modern brains can't tell the difference between a real or imagined threats, so we worry regardless. For most of us, our day-to-day lives don't include confrontations or life and death situations involving animals that want to rip us to shreds. So all this worrying is useless.

The only time worrying is helpful is when it spurs you into action

Instead of worrying, use your brain to change your thought processes or take the actions that you need to take to solve a problem. Most worries are not this type. Most worries are fed by doubt and fear. They show up as questions like "What if I fail at this?", "What if I bottle it?", "What if I'm not good enough?... Strong enough?... Young enough?..."

What to Do

1. Sometimes, all it takes is to tell your worries to get lost or to feck off. Ask yourself, what are your constant worries? Do you worry a lot about the possibilities of this bad thing happening or that worse thing happening? Are you afraid to do things in your life because you can't predict the outcome? We never worry about things going right, it's always about what might go wrong. We use this fantastic brain of ours to conjure up images and realities that we don't want. What a waste of time! Tell your worries to take a back seat. Everything you will ever do in your life starts out as a thought in your mind, everything.

Remember the Nikos Kazantzakis quote from earlier: "By believing passionately in that which doesn't exist, you create it and that which has not been sufficiently desired is what we call the non-existent." Use it to conjure up positive, inspiring images and realities, not negativity. The more you train your mind to think confidently about who you are and where you're going, the more building blocks you'll put down to construct that same positive reality.

2. Rejoice in your imperfections. Nobody is perfect. Life is messy by nature, for all of us. Some things go right, other things go wrong. You need to accept that your life is not going to be perfect. You are going to experience your share of perfect moments. The more constructively you think, the more of these moments you'll have. But you are unlikely to find many of them if you sit around wallowing in your self-driven worry.

3. Listen out for your Gollum. We all have an inner voice that's only happy when you're smack-bang in the middle of your comfort zone, forever. The Gollum doesn't like getting too close to the edge of that comfort zone. If you get too close, it might put big thoughts into your head which could cause you to take a step too far. That means only one thing, more discomfort.

Have you ever stood too close to the edge of a cliff and wondered what it would be like to jump? It doesn't mean you're suicidal, it's just a brief image that's projected to your consciousness to scare you into backing off. Richard Bandler, one of the founders of NLP, tells a story of a woman who had a phobia of high places. He asked her what was happening in her mind as she approached the edge of a tall building or cliff. After a bit of coaxing, she said it was like a movie was being played out in her mind, of her jumping off the edge and smashing to bloody pieces on the ground far below. She visualized all the blood and gore and broken bones, her head bursting open like a ripe melon. He said no wonder she was petrified. He would be too. She wasn't afraid of the height, she was scared to death of smashing to pieces because of the fall. What if one day she actually jumped off? He told her to stop playing the movie and replace it with a movie of herself being relaxed and comfortable, staying away from the edge.

Your Gollum will try to talk you into doing nothing, staying away from the edge of your comfort zone and to not even think about changing. It will plead with you to stay within what you know, 'What's wrong with the way we've always done things', it will ask. It will tell you you're not good enough, you don't deserve any success, or you're just not the right type of person for this sort of thing. Don't listen to the Gollum. It will hold you back. The only place where you can ever positively change is outside of your comfort zone. So tell your Gollum to be quiet. Tell your worries to feck off.

65. On Your Own for the Night? Why Not Masturdate!

Let me say that word again, masturdate... as in master date! Masturdating is a comical modern term used for taking yourself out on a date. As funny as it sounds, temporary solitude is very beneficial in your life, it's good to be in your own company once in a while. The word masturdate has been coined because a person who is out and about on their own is often viewed as sad or somehow pathetic, particularly if they're sat in a restaurant, a movie theater, or some other setting where the norm is sociability.

What's the big problem? People find no problem if you sit in a coffee shop on your own, or in a fast food joint, what's the big deal about being in a restaurant on your own.

My life is filled with people who I love to be with, my partner, my family, and my close friends, and it would be very empty without them. We get together as often as we can, that's a part of a normal life.

But sometimes I like to get away on my own. I'm an introvert by nature so I really don't mind my own company. I like the chance to get away from my normal surroundings, it helps me to think straight and to put my thoughts straight. So, getting away from everyone else when I feel the need for some chill out time is something I do quite often. It helps me to bring balance in my life. It also helps me to be sociable when I'm with other people, to bring out the extrovert in myself. As you know, I like walking, and that fulfills my solitude needs to a certain degree. But sometimes I want to be on my own and have a meal.

What to Do

1. First choose your masturdating venue or activity. It doesn't have to be sitting alone in a restaurant or cinema. Just use your imagination. Hire a car at a racing circuit. Go pony trekking. Take a parachute. Get a massage. Go for a spa treatment.

2. Don't feel guilty about it. Sometimes your life just has to be about you and you alone.

3. If you're going to the cinema, theater, or some other auditorium event, choose an aisle seat so you won't be disturbing anyone else if you decide to move or leave. And there's less likelihood that you'll get caught between two canoodling couples.

4. If you're going to a restaurant on your own, take a book. It looks way more sophisticated if you're reading rather than flicking through your phone, which just looks like you've been stood-up.

5. Most importantly, set out with the intention and expectation that you are going to thoroughly enjoy yourself.

66. Take a Loopy Leaf from the Japanese Book of Relaxation

Now we're going to take a step right out of the box and look at some of the strange methods the Japanese are using to relax and relieve their stress. Japan is a country full of worrywarts, so it comes as no surprise to me that they have a multitude of weird and wonderful ways of relaxing or relieving stress.

Asian counties have some of the highest stress levels on the planet. For the Japanese, going on vacation is not about relaxing on the beach, building sandcastles, and enjoying the freedom to do nothing as they watch the sunset slipping below the horizon. The Japanese like to vacation like busy bees, flitting from one thing to another and visiting everything that can be visited. If they're not doing that, they're shopping or taking photographing everything in sight.

When I was doing the research for *Hang Loose Without Booze*, I came across some of the strangest methods of relaxation that I've ever heard of, most of them hailing from Japan. I couldn't resist doing a section about this...

What Do They Do?

Here's some of the funny and loopy methods the Japanese have come up with to relieve their stress.

1. The Japanese Shouting Vase

This is a vase-shaped implement which is meant to hold your anger. You build your lungs to capacity, put one end of the vase to your lips, and scream into it with all your might. What comes out the other end is a mere whisper. You can find this 'pot of screaming' on Amazon here: http://www.amazon.com/Stress-Reduction-Japanese-Shouting-Holds/dp/B001H5Q3BW

2. The Unani Technique

The Unani technique is a form of traditional medicine which is practiced in South Asia and the Middle East. Unani is based on the teachings of Galen and Hippocrates and centers around the concept of the four humors: Blagham (Phlegm), Dam (Blood), Ṣafrā' (Yellow Bile), and Saudā' (Black Bile). Treatment involves leech therapy.

3. Electronic Bubble Wrap

Do you remember a time, a few years ago, when people were touting the wonders of bubble wrap for stress relief? The Japanese have gone one step further and invented an electronic version. Of course they did, who else! This mad version has many sonic variations including the traditional pop, a doorbell, dog bark, and the sound of a whip. Because it's electronic, you'll never run out of pops. http://www.amazon.com/Thumbsup-Bubble-Wrap-Keychain/dp/B00W3TCACC/ref=sr_1_2?ie=UTF8&qid=14376409 28&sr=8-2&keywords=electronic+bubble+wrap

4. Smash Some Plates

We've all seen the scenario of someone taking out their anger by throwing something breakable across the room. There's a taste of frustration in the home air, the tension rises to a peak, and all of a sudden there's crockery and delph flying around like a bad remake of Poltergeist. In Japan, one entrepreneur has taken this plate smashing to the next level by starting a business where you can smash plates to your hearts content. *The Venting Place* is all about getting rid of your frustrations in one massive release of porcelain. You simply go in, don your protective gear, and start throwing your ceramics. He charges by the plate, of course!

5. Maggot Alien Head

You've heard of the stress ball, right? When you're stressed, you take one of these pliable balls in your hand and squeeze it until you feel relief. In Japan, they've gone one step further and added a bit of creepy humor in the form of a maggoty alien stress head. You still squeeze the ball to release your frustrations, but instead of squeezing until you feel better, you squeeze until the fun sized rubber maggots pop out of its eyeballs.

67. Where Words Fail, Music Speaks

Music has a very unique place in our emotions. When you listen to one type of music, you want to dance, listen to another and you want to cry. Music can induce your mind and body to relax, to become mindful, or even to sleep. Billy Joel said, "I think music in itself is healing. It's an explosive expression of humanity. It's something we are all touched by. No matter what culture we're from, everyone loves music." And Beethoven had this to say, "Music is the mediator between the spiritual and the sensual life."

Over the centuries, there has been mountains of research into the power of music. Some studies have looked at how listening to music on headphones can reduce stress levels of patients who're about to undergo surgery and after surgery to aid recovery. Listening to music has been proved to increase positive feelings and reduce depression. The wrong type of music can do the reverse. You don't need anyone to tell you how music can alter your moods. We all do it. We all feel the effects. Music can help to bring stability and order into the lives of children suffering from severe physical or mental disabilities. And you can use music to change your mood almost instantly.

For me, one of the most touching demonstrations of the power of music to alter emotions came from the eminent author and neurologist Dr. Oliver Sacks. He said, "Music can do things which language can't. When we use music therapy with Alzheimer's patients, something very powerful and primal is at work." In an article on Oprah.com*, Dr. Sacks said, "I have seen this over and over again in my practice as a neurologist. The right sort of music can literally unlock someone frozen by Parkinson's disease, so that they may be able to dance or sing, even though, in the absence of music, they may be unable to take a step or say a word." There is a wonderful video on YouTube about an elderly gentleman called Henry Graham. Henry is an Alzheimer's patient who doesn't even recognize his own daughter. But watch his reaction as the staff put a pair of headphones over his ears and play music from his own era...Warning, watching this video may cause a tear or two - it did from me!

What to Do

1. Start your day with some pleasant, soft music. Have you ever seen a sunrise over the ocean on a cloudless morning? It doesn't just pop up, it's a gradual process from darkness to daylight. First there's a barely perceptible illumination in the sky. Gradually, the day gets brighter and brighter. Just before the earth spins around to meet the sun, the sky starts to redden. Daylight itself happens long before the sun actually shows its face. Then, like an explosion over the horizon, the sun shows its morning face and continues on its slow progress across the day. How ordinary would the start of the day be if the sun just appeared as if some celestial switch had been flipped over? That's exactly what you do when you blast yourself with an alarm clock every morning or turn on the TV to watch a never-ending stream of pandemonium. Instead, you should imitate the sun and gradually raise yourself to the day with some soft and soothing music. Use the playlist function on your iPod to create a wake-up inspirational music stream to gently pace you into your day.

2. Use the power of music to move you. Earlier on, I talked about motion creating and changing emotion. When you do your morning exercise routine, harness the natural primal nature of music to rock your senses, move your body and soul, and eliminate your tensions and stress. By the way, you're missing out on something special if you don't have a morning exercise routine. You need to gift yourself some quality movement time in the morning. It pulls you into the swing of the day, gets the exercise out of the way, and sets your mood standard for everything that follows.

3. Use the power of music to move those around you. Listening to music while you're on your own has many, many benefits. You take it to another level when you listen to, or play your music, with a group of other people. That's why night clubs, or discos as I'd call them, are so important. Watch people who dance, all frowns disappear and the smiles light up everyone's faces.

*http://www.oprah.com/health/Oliver-Sacks-Finds-the-Bond-Between-Music-and-Our-Brains

68. Sing Like No One's Listening!

Another fantastic way that you can chill out with music is to create your own. Sing, even if you don't consider yourself to be a very good singer. Placedo Domingo once said, "Singing is a form of therapy". A common theme for *Hang Loose Without Booze* is your ability to easily elevate your good emotions, that it's your choice to do so. Here's another way, through singing. Singing motivates your body to relax, it helps you to strengthen your lungs in the long-term, and breathe more deeply in the short-term. Ella Fitzgerald said, "The only thing better than singing is more singing".

Singing as part of a group can bring even more benefits. According to Swedish scientists, people who sing in a choir become so in tune with each other that their hearts begin to beat in synchronization. If that's true, it's amazing. These scientists, from the University of Gothenburg, asked a group of teenagers to hum, sing, and finally chant. They found that when the students sang, the effect on their heart variability was striking. The leader of the study, Dr. Björn Vickhoff told the UKs Telegraph newspaper*, "Song is a form of regular, controlled breathing, since breathing out occurs on the song phrases and inhaling takes place between these. It gives you pretty much the same effect as yoga breathing. It helps you relax, and there are indications that it does provide a heart benefit."

What to Do

1. Don't worry if you think you can't sing, that's not really the point. If you're singing on your own, nobody except you can hear. If they do hear you singing, so what, it makes you sound like you're having fun.

2. Sing whenever you feel like it... in the shower, on the way to work, while out walking. I love to sing when I have the house to myself, belting out a few verses of whatever song I'm in the mood for.

3. Join a singing group. As you can see from the Gothenburg study, singing in a group can give you extra benefits. Find a choir. It could be religious or secular. Search the internet for opportunities to join a group. Look in your local newspaper. Or just ask around.

*http://www.telegraph.co.uk/news/health/10168914/All-together-now-singing-is-good-for-your-body-and-soul.html

69. The Scientific 7 Minute Workout for Immediate Benefits

Most people's experience with exercising involves finding excuses not to do it. And one of the biggest excuses is that there's just no time. Time shouldn't be a factor. You can get the greatest positive impact and benefit by doing short burst interval training.

According to Brett Klika and Chris Jordan at the Human Performance Institute of Orlando, Florida, high-intensity circuit training (HICT) using only body weight as resistance, combining aerobic and resistance training into a single exercise, and only lasting 7 minutes, can "deliver numerous health benefits in much less time than traditional programs". One of the immediate benefits from this type of concise exercise is less stress and more relaxation.

What to Do

Before I give you the exercises in the basic training session, let me first explain how it works.

The key is in the word 'interval'.

Between each high intensity exercise, you need to rest for ten seconds. This gives your body a chance to recover.

Then you alternate between muscles to extend the recovery period.

You begin exercising the muscles in the upper body, rest, and then work out the lower body. This allows one set of large muscles to 'rest' while working out the other set. To get the full benefit of the workout, follow the sequence as laid out below. Each exercise should be done for 30 seconds. 30 seconds on, 10 seconds off, 30 seconds on, 10 seconds off...and so on.

The Exercises

1. Jumping jacks
https://www.youtube.com/watch?v=c4DAnQ6DtF8

2. Wall sit
https://www.youtube.com/watch?v=XULOKw4E4P4

3. Push-ups
https://www.youtube.com/watch?v=Q7cPaJZoOng

4. Abdominal crunches
https://www.youtube.com/watch?v=2yOFvV-NSeY

5. Step-ups onto a chair
https://www.youtube.com/watch?v=aajhW7DD1EA

6. Squats   https://www.youtube.com/watch?v=UXJrBgI2RxA

7. Triceps dip from a chair
https://www.youtube.com/watch?v=6kALZikXxLc

8. Plank   https://www.youtube.com/watch?v=pSHjTRCQxIw

9. High knees running in place
https://www.youtube.com/watch?v=dt7FAEYRLC4

10. Lunge
https://www.youtube.com/watch?v=QF0BQS2W80k

11. Push-ups and rotation
https://www.youtube.com/watch?v=o2Qek4N2ea8

12. Side plank
https://www.youtube.com/watch?v=6cRAFji80CQ

You can find an online interval timer at:
www.intervaltimer.com

70. It's All in Your Hands

If everyone had access to their own private masseuse or spa center whenever they felt the slightest twinge of tension, the world would be a much happier place. Unfortunately, that lifestyle is reserved for the lucky few. That's life! Even if you're denied the benefits of some warm, soft, massaging hands at the drop of a hat, you can always give your own hands a good massage. Self-hand massaging techniques are very easy to learn, simple to perform provided you take one hand at a time, and they are completely free - apart from the small cost for your preferred massage lotion.

These hand massaging techniques have been adapted from reflexology. These massages will soothe any tension in your hands, help you to feel relaxed, and create some serenity in your day. If you carry a small bottle of lotion in your pocket or your handbag, you can give yourself a quick hand massage whenever you have a free five minutes. Often, five minutes of focused therapy is all it takes to help you to relax and unwind.

What to Do

1. When you choose a lotion, try to find one that's hydrating and nourishing. A pleasant smelling lotion will also help soothe your mind.

2. Start with the heels of your hands. Using the thumb of your right hand and begin massaging some lotion into the heel of your left hand, working your way from the outside in, the part furthest from your thumb. Use circular motions to gradually work the cream into the muscle, easing any tension.

3. After you have finished with the heel, move to the muscle

web between the thumb and forefinger. This part of the hand takes a lot of punishment as it stretches back and forth through the day. Grasp the skin of your left hand between the thumb and forefinger of your right hand and gently massage up and down, backwards and forwards.

4. Now switch your attention to your left palm. Gently rub your thumb backwards and forwards along your palm from the heel to your fingers. Then spend a little time with each joint at the base of each finger.

5. Flip your left hand over and start on the back. This is a whole hand massage, so let's not leave anything out. Again, moving from the bottom to the top of your hand, massage along and between the bones, from the wrist to the knuckles. Apply as much pressure as you can take without causing pain.

6. Now it's time to move onto your fingers. There are several ways to massage your fingers. One method is to take each finger of your left hand and completely encase it in the palm of your right hand. Gently pull and twist, making sure to flex the joints back and forth. Never strain too hard. Another method is to take each finger of your left hand between the thumb and forefinger of your right and flex backwards and forwards, contracting and extending the finger, while gently rubbing the skin.

7. Repeat steps 2 through 6 with your right hand.

71. The Best of Three Sets - Tennis Ball Massage

Anyone for tennis? All you need are some green furry balls for this relaxation technique.

Tennis ball massage is a form of DIY massage that can help you to release tight muscles in your back and other hard-to-get-to areas of your body. It's free, if you steal the tennis ball, you can do it almost anywhere, although privacy is best, and it works really well.

By the way, what color is a tennis ball? I think they're yellow, my partner calls them green! Maybe they're yellowish green? Greenish-yellow? Did you know that puzzles are good for calming the nerves as well?

Like all massage, these techniques are meant to be releasing and relaxing, not painful. Although there's a fine line between pain and comfort in massage. When you're on the receiving end of a deep massage, you know there's bad pain and good pain. The good pain is where it hurts but you don't want the therapist to stop. Don't apply so much pressure that it gets painful, only sufficient so the pain is comfortably bearable. That's one of the benefits of self-massage, you can tell instantly if it's getting too painful and back off. A therapist has to wait for the client's response, usually a yelp, before they can judge if they're digging too deep.

Here's the three techniques:

What to Do
1. Tennis Ball Foot

Remove your shoes. Sit in a comfortable chair with your back straight. Place a tennis ball under one foot at a time, focusing the pressure on one specific area. Once you get used to it, you can use one ball under each foot. Roll your foot over the ball from front to back and back to front. For areas that feel extra tight, hold the ball in that area and apply consistent pressure for thirty seconds to a full minute.

2. Tennis Ball Back

Stand with your back to a wall. Place the tennis ball between your back and the wall. Apply consistent pressure, moving the tennis ball across your back from one side to the other. Now bend your legs up and down as you move the ball lengthwise from top to bottom.

3. Tennis Ball Back 2

Find a comfortable area to lie down. Place the tennis ball under your lower back, to the right of your spine. Now just relax. Allow gravity to do it's job, slowly lowering your back onto the ball, letting the ball squeeze your lower back muscles. After a couple of moments, move the ball a little higher on your back, still keeping it to the right of your spine. Relax again and let gravity to its work. After a couple more moments, move the ball up again and continue to massage until you reach your shoulders. Now switch the ball over to the left hand side of your spine and work your way down and repeat the pattern outlined above.

Other Tennis Ball Massage Techniques:

https://www.youtube.com/watch?v=bjnu1liKoDE

https://www.youtube.com/watch?v=6uhRgaaojaw

https://www.youtube.com/watch?v=6L3VLrdXWho

72. If Your Feet are Happy You are Happy!

Again, as with hand massage, giving your feet the benefit of a quick massage is one of the easiest forms of self-massage and can do wonders for your lowering stress levels and bringing about relaxation.

It's easy to just sit down, pull one foot onto your knee and start rubbing. You'll find way more value if you put a bit more attention into your surroundings, making your foot massage a treat. It's a simple thing to sit comfortably, light a candle and a joss stick, play some chill-out sounds, set up your mood. Let everyone else know you're giving yourself a few minutes of pampering and you don't want to be disturbed.

This is nothing new to the women out there. Women seem to know instinctively how to create mood. But the lads might need a bit more coaxing. It's not something that comes naturally, I know. When a man does this kind of thing, lighting the candles and making the room smell nice with joss sticks, it feels very feminine, very girly, and that's not good for the masculine ego. My advice, let it go! It's all in the head. If all you do is spend five minutes massaging your feet with some oil, you're feet are going thank you for it, no doubt about it. But if that's all you do, you're missing an important element from the whole experience, something much deeper and longer lasting.

The music and lighting and aromas are all there to create an expectation. When you've done this for a while, lighting the joss sticks and the candles, putting on the contemplative music, your brain and body will start to respond, these things become automatic triggers for you to relax, even before you start massaging. The same goes with meditation. Everything is set up in such a way that it becomes familiar, the way the room looks, feels, and smells. Sitting in the same position. Chanting the same thing over and over. It's all designed to say to your brain, right - this is meditation time - let's relax.

The more you put your body and mind into this environment, following the same pattern, firing off the same relaxation triggers, the quicker your body will start to respond. It won't happen the first time because your mind and body don't really know what's happening or what to expect. The more you do this, paying attention to the details, the more these practices become habitual. The more habitual they become, the more you'll get out of it. Your body will know what to expect and respond very quickly - yay, it's relaxation time!

Let's look at the massage.

What to Do

1. Take a bowl of warm water and give your feet a pre-pampering cleanse.

2. Wipe your feet dry with a towel.

3. Take some of your favorite massage oil and apply to your feet. You could try almond or sesame seed oil blended with some lavender essential oil.

4. Choose one foot and begin your massage at the little toe.

5. Massage the base of the toe and gently flex the joints of as you rub in the oil.

6. Move along to the next toe. First concentrate your massage on the webbing between the two toes, then move to the toe itself.

7. Follow this procedure for the next toes, beginning your massage between the toes, then focusing on the toe itself.

8. Now move backwards to the ball of your foot. Apply pressure with your fingers and thumb, making small circular

movements and making sure you work out the whole ball.

9. Repeat the same process with the rest of your foot.

10. After you have finished with kneading the base of your heel, move up to the sides and focus your massage just below the ankle.

11. Massage your ankle using gentle pressure.

12. You can finish up by rubbing some more oil into your calf muscle to release any built-up tension.

13. Move to the other foot and repeat the process.

73. Let it Come, Let it Go, Let it Flow - DIY Accupressure

Acupressure is an ancient Chinese practice that is sometimes referred to as acupuncture without the needles. Acupressure works by applying pressure to the body's meridians, which are the energy channels which transport the life energy or qi. Acupressure practitioners use the fingers, hands, feet, elbows, or special devices to exert this pressure. It is used for medicinal purposes and for promoting health and well-being in the patient.

Some people believe that acupressure is capable of treating problems with the mind, emotions, and spirit. They also support that acupressure works by releasing muscle tension, stimulating the body's natural pain killers such as endorphins, and improving the circulation. As well as therapy, acupressure points are studied and used by many martial arts as a way of incapacitating or controlling an opponent.

Acupressure is very safe. If you're going to employ the services of an acupressure professional, always choose a licensed practitioner to be sure of this safety aspect and to get the best value for your money.

You don't have to go to a professional to get the benefits of acupressure. Here are a few simple techniques that you can use on yourself.

What to Do

1. The Temple Press

Use your middle fingers to press on the temples. This will

help to promote relaxation, decrease stress, and relieve headaches.

2. The Third Eye Press

Press your finger on the point between your eyebrows, known as the middle eye. You can also gently tap at that point.

3. The Inner Eye Press

Press your fingers gently at the point where your eyes meet your nose. You often see people doing this with one hand, pinching between the finger and thumb. You can either follow this or press the points with your two index fingers.

4. The Cupid's Bow Press

Press your finger on the point between the bottom of your nose and the top of your upper lip. Hold for a couple of minutes or until you feel discomfort.

5. The Chin Press

Another spot for you to experiment with is the point just below your lower lip and above your chin.

6. The Wrist Press

Clench your fist so the tendons on the palm-side of your wrist stand up. Now measure two thumb widths upwards from the skin crease at the join between your hand and lower arm. Relax your arm as you apply pressure with your thumb nail. Apply only enough pressure until you feel a slight but comfortable pain. While you are maintaining the pressure, make slow kneading motions. Continue for about one minute. Repeat with the other hand.

7. The Foot Press

Sit on a chair or the side of your bed. Lift your foot onto your knee so you can see the sole of the foot. The pressure point can be found about one third down from your toes, just below the ball of the foot. Again, you should only press hard enough to cause a slight, but comfortable pain. Continue for one to two minutes.

8. The Ear Rub

Sit in a comfortable position, with your back straight,

somewhere you can remain quiet and undisturbed. Use the outside of your fingers and your thumbs to gently massage your ears, pulling them outwards. You can also use your fingertips to rub down the insides of your ears, getting into every fold and tracing every ridge.

74. Wash Away Your Troubles With a Bath Full of Bubbles

The only time I take a bath is when there's no shower available. I should take them more often because the hot water and soap always make me feel much calmer, happy, and physically relaxed. But having a bath takes a long time, I've things to get on with, to I prefer to hop into the shower and be done with it.

Having said that, there's lot to be said for multi-tasking. I listen to audiobooks and podcasts when I walk, or do the dishes, or when I'm cooking. So I guess I could do the same while taking a bath.

I still have a lot of reframing to do. Instead of looking at taking a bath as primarily for cleaning my body, I could reframe the whole experience as primarily for relaxing my body, and getting clean and fresh as a bonus. I said in the last section that I think most men, especially older men, have a problem with the whole concept of pampering. Taking a bath to feel good, to get that feeling of smooth glowing skin, to smell good, or to feel rejuvenated is just not part of manly vocabulary. But it's all in the head. In reality, there's no place where it says you can still do an Ironman and come home to a bubble bath. These things are not mutually exclusive. There's enough room for discipline and for pampering. At the end of the day, it all boils down to using the tools that you have, to get to the place where you want to go, without the need to poison your system with alcohol. If that means taking a bubble bath, so be it, I'm all for up that.

What to Do

Firstly, you should engineer the atmosphere to get the best out of your best relaxation experience. Dim the lighting, use some joss sticks or scented candles, add some oils and herbs to the water, and approach it with expectations that you are going to feel relaxed and happy.

1. Relax. Be mindful of the water, or how you are feeling. As you soak in the bath, go through some of the other relaxation techniques in *Hang Loose Without Booze*. I tend to try and fill every waking moment with mental stimulation. If I am not reading, I am looking at emails or surfing the web. I've had to teach myself that relaxing and letting my mind wander is also a part of a healthy life. If you have to read, choose something light, material that doesn't need much concentration.

2. You deserve and need to be pampered every so often. If you lay in the bath, but think your problems and worries or the mountain of tasks that are facing you in your life, you won't fully relax. If you lay there thinking you should be doing something else instead of pampering yourself, the benefit will be lost.

3. Aromatherapy. One of the other techniques that I've written about in these books is using your sense of smell to relax. Aromatherapy is a fancy way of saying that you light some scented candles or joss sticks to engineer the right mood.

4. Bath Salts/Herbs/Salt/Seaweed. Adding these things to your bath gives you another dimension for relaxation and healing. Some soothe the tension away. Others promote your circulation.

5. Candles. Candles provide a soft background for your relaxation.

6. How long should you bathe? You might be tempted to hop out of the bath after ten minutes. Don't do it. Keep soaking up the energy, the salts, the fragrances. Relax for at least twenty minutes to feel the full benefits.

75. La Hora de la Siesta

Since moving to Spain, I've adopted quite a few Spanish cultural practices, none with so much gusto. I've found that taking a siesta is a fantastic way of revitalizing my energies for the second half of my day. Winston Churchill was another siesta partaker, he said that he adopted the habit while in Cuba and it has allowed him to work 1.5 days in every 24 hours.

In Ireland, the siesta is known as taking an afternoon nap, but unless I was dying with a hangover, a nap was something you did when you were a young kid or an old man. Again, it wasn't very manly to sleep during the day. It meant there was something wrong with you.

I believe in seizing the moment because this is all you ever really get. So it's hard to put everything down and go for a sleep halfway through the day. But since I've integrated the siesta into my day, I feel like I just function a lot better. One hour of concentrated rest is better than three hours of unrested toil.

Why does the siesta work so well for us humans? Generally, human sleep follows a monophasic pattern. This means that our 24 hour day is split into two sections, one for being awake, another for being asleep. Most other species of mammal follow a polyphasic sleep pattern, which means that they sleep for short periods spaced out throughout their day. There have been several studies that show that taking regular siestas not only improves your long-term alertness, memory, and creativity, it can help your cardiovascular system and reduce stress, making you feel more relaxed.

What to Do

1. A siesta is more beneficial if you nap on a couch or on a reclining chair of some sort, not in your bed. When you lay down in your regular bed your brain associates it with regular sleep. This can trigger your brain to go into a deeper sleep. This is not a siesta. A short snooze will reinvigorate you. When you wake you'll feel refreshed and ready to go. If you fall into a deeper sleep, you'll wake feeling groggy. Deep sleep during the day could also interfere with your night time sleeping.

2. How long should you sleep? A snooze should last no more than half an hour. The American space agency, NASA, has found that the optimum span for your siesta is 26 minutes.

3. The Different Types of Napping.

There are three basic types of siesta.

The Planned Siesta

The planned siesta is a way of delaying your regular sleep time. If you think you're going to be awake later than normal, let's say you're attending a party or some other event that extends beyond your bedtime, you can mitigate any sleep loss by having a nap earlier in the day.

The Emergency Siesta

The emergency siesta is in response to feeling tired in the moment. When you feel tired in the normal course of your day, you take a nap in an attempt to boost your energy and your levels of concentration.

The Habitual Siesta

The habitual siesta is the type found in countries like Spain where a person takes a nap at the same time each and every day. During the summer months, the siesta is not only taken to refresh the body and rejuvenate the mind, it's a way of dealing with the high summer temperatures. Many shops and businesses close during the hours of 3pm and 5pm, much longer than the 15 to 30 minutes it takes for a traditional siesta.

4. How do you take your siesta? Find somewhere you're not likely to be disturbed. Close your eyes and doze off for no more than 30 minutes. Set an alarm if you need to. Don't forget to turn your phone to silent. I turn mine off for that period because even the vibration will bring me out of my light snooze. Take your siesta at the same time each day.

76. The Best Meditation - Sleep

"Sleep is the best meditation."

Dalai Lama

Getting a good night's sleep is essential for maintaining the balance between your mind and body and your life. For some people who've just quit drinking, finding sleep is not as easy as it sounds. The body of a drinker is used to having the alcohol flowing. Even though alcohol is a poison, your body doesn't know you're drinking it on purpose, and it will be doing its best to work around the toxin, trying to keep everything in some sort of balance, however distorted that balance is.

Everything changes when you quit. This distorted balance is suddenly turned upside down and your system yet isn't set up to deal with that. Your body doesn't see the alcohol as alcohol, it sees it as a threat, pure and simple. When you fall asleep really quickly from a lot of booze, that's not the alcohol, it's your body getting you out of the way, with all your movement and talking and falling down, so it can deal with this immediate threat to your existence. Putting you unconscious means your body can concentrate much more of its precious resources on eliminating the poison and keeping you alive. When you think you're having a good night's sleep after drinking a load of booze, resting up your body for the next day, think again! Your body is continuing to work furiously in the background.

And don't forget that we put most of this poison into our body in the evenings. By the time you get into your bed and your body forces you into unconsciousness, this is when the accumulation of alcohol and the threat to your life is at its highest. How can we ever think that this is a situation where our body is going to be relaxed? How can we ever think that we are getting the rest that our body and mind need to function properly? The reality is that during these first few hours of unconsciousness, your body is struggling to cope with the onslaught. Why do you think you are always so tired in the mornings? This is something you only realize when you haven't been drinking for a while, when the poisoning has stopped.

As I said, once the alcohol flow stops, after your system realizes that the threat has passed, your body will start rebalancing itself, readjusting to the new situation. But this takes time. It's not going to happen in one or two days, it could take a week or even a month.

Apart from insignificant traces, all the alcohol will be gone from your system within those first couple of days, but your body's expectation of more alcohol will take longer to filter out. Your body operates in the real world, it's not swayed by your fickleness or fancy, it doesn't care what might be happening or what your plans are, it's only concerned with what's happening right now at this moment. It's like a soldier on the battlefield who has to deal with the situation as it is and as that situation is unfolding. The military top brass have their plans, the way they want the battle to play out, but the soldier has to go with what is happening in the real world.

It's the same thing with your own defense system. Just because you are saying that there will be no more alcohol, that there's never going to be any more alcohol, and that you want your life to change for the better, your body only operates on what's happening right now, on what it knows the situation to be. The current situation is that toxins are still in your system and there's the assumption that even though the flow might have stopped, based on past experience the likelihood is that the flow is going to resume. So your body is going to stay on alert for a while.

You are stuck between the old situation, your drinking, and the new situation, you leading a healthier life. So for the first few days, you are stuck in this limbo. You're no longer drinking, but you haven't yet reached the place of not-drinking. You will get there, it just takes time.

Troubled sleeping was one of my only problems when I stopped drinking. In those first couple of nights, I tossed and turned, not really getting any proper sleep. I think I dozed for a while each night. Once my body gradually became accustomed to not having alcohol, my sleep improved. It took about a month before my sleeping patterns had really stabilized, and by then I was getting the best sleeps that I'd had in a long time.

Why did I have trouble sleeping?

First, as I wrote about earlier, my body was in this limbo. It's a sort of demilitarized zone. The toxins have stopped their onslaught but the ceasefire is not yet guaranteed. So everything is still on alert, at DefCon 4 instead of DefCon 5.

Second, because I'd quit drinking 5 years previously, and I'd had trouble sleeping back then, my expectation was of this repeating itself. Memory is never 20/20, so I didn't recall how lon lg the insomnia lasted or how severe it was. But my expectations certainly affected the reality of what actually happened. I was subconsciously telling myself that I wasn't going to sleep in the first few days, based on my past experience, and guess what happened.

The third reason I found it difficult to sleep was because I hadn't yet established a bedtime routine for my new life. I went straight from my body knocking me out at night so it could deal with the toxic threat, to relying on my body to relax under its own steam.

I was also going from being fully active, feeling that I had loads of energy without the booze, to trying to sleep. The human body doesn't respond well under those circumstances. It needs a certain amount time to prepare for bed. That means more than just putting on your pajamas and turning the lights off. For at least an hour before you go to bed, your body has to wind down.

I talk about plenty of relaxation techniques in *Hang Loose*

Without Booze... We'll go over a couple of simple routines below.

How much sleep do you need?

People differ depending on their age, size and weight, their level of activity and stress during the day, their diet, and so on. Common medical recommendations for how much sleep you need fluctuate between 7 and 9 hours per night, depending on who you ask. In my opinion, you should aim at a happy medium of 8 hours every night. Try to stabilize going to bed and getting up again in the morning to the same times each day. Your body loves habit and consistency. I've woken up at 6 every morning for as long as I can remember, regardless of what time I go to sleep. I normally start getting ready for bed around 9pm and try to be asleep by 10.

What to Do

1. Start getting ready for bed roughly an hour before you actually lie down.

2. Use some of the relaxation techniques found throughout *Hang Loose Without Booze*.

3. Dim the lights and turn off the TV.

4. Don't use your bedroom for anything else but sleep (and sex, of course). Your bedroom should be a place where your body switches to relaxation and sleep automatically. That means no television, no computers, no mobile phones. I cheat a little with the last one because reading novels has always been a part of my bedtime routine. I've switched to reading on my phone at night because it's easier to hold. I turn down the phone's backlight so I'm not disturbed too much.

5. If you're thinking worried thoughts before you go to sleep or if you just can't get rid of a pesky thought that seems to want to dance around in your brain, take a couple of minutes to write it down on a piece of paper. Then throw the paper away. A clear mind will help you sleep better.

6. Breathe yourself into slumber. Take some deep breathes to relax. Deep breathing sparks your parasympathetic system, which is similar to the effect produced by yawning. You can also use

visualizations. Yawning is infectious, so if you make a picture in your mind of someone else yawning, it should be enough to get you yawning as well.

77. Would You Like One Can of Whoop Ass or Two?

Some people insist that an ass whooping never solved anything. I think it all depends on the ass whooping. Hitting out at a person is not going to solve anything and will probably get you in trouble in more ways than one. But I can think of no better way of releasing your pent up energy than pounding away at a gym bag for five or ten minutes.

Of course, if you are feeling anger or frustration or pent-up energy, you need to deal with the underlying causes. No amount of beating up on a punch bag is going to cure your problems. But it might just reduce the levels of these emotions so you can deal with your difficulties in a more calm and measured manner.

How do you get set up for gym bag ass whooping? The immediate solution is to join a boxing gym or some other place with such a set-up. You'll have access to all their equipment and you can punch away to your heart's content. You might even like to have a go putting some ass whooping onto a real live person in a one-on-one sparring session.

Alternatively, you can buy a punch bag for using in your own home. These bags are relatively inexpensive. I found one on Amazon.com for about $25. You'll need a strong anchor point on a ceiling to hang the bag. If you can't do this, you can also purchase a gym bag stand. There are only a couple of other things you'll need to get you started. Half-finger boxing gloves cost less than $10. Again, I found a pair on Amazon for just over $6. You'll also need some hand wrap. As you can see, you don't need a lot of money to set yourself up.

What to Do

1. The most important thing is not to do any damage to yourself or to anyone else. So preparation is essential before you start to box.

2. Your hands and wrists are going to take most of the impact, so this is the area you need to concentrate your preparations. Wrap your hands first. There are a lot of YouTube video tutorials showing you how to do this properly. The main thing is to wrap your hands tightly. If your hands are moving around inside your gloves while you're boxing, you're doing it wrong and you risk damage.

3. Before you start boxing, do a quick warm up. All it takes is a couple of minutes doing jumping jacks or running on the spot.

4. When you start boxing, aim your punches at the center of the bag which tends to be the softest part.

5. Start off your boxing sessions with one minute rounds, then take a break. Work your way up to 3 minutes per round.

6. If you want to start boxing before your equipment arrives, or you don't want to actually hit anything, shadow boxing can be a good alternative. You don't get the satisfying smack at the end of the punch, but you'll certainly burn a lot of calories and release some tension. Make sure you don't overextend your arms while shadow boxing which can cause problems for your elbow joints.

78. Snap Yourself Out of It!

Your thoughts are the birthplace for all your stressed out feelings. When you're quitting drinking, for instance, it's easy to get caught up in the 'woe-is-me' thought patterns that focus your attention on the discomfort you feel right now and forgetting about the reasons why you quit in the first place.

Before I quit, I was having the most awful hangovers that had started to last two or even three days. I felt physically exhausted, my body ached all the time, and my life seemed to be going nowhere fast. When I stopped drinking, I didn't go through any really horrible symptoms. Quite the opposite. Without the alcohol poisoning my body any more I felt exhilarated.

I'd be lying if I said I didn't have my moments of glorified moaning, but I always managed to talk myself down. In those moaning moments, I had to speak to myself like I was a child, reassuring and encouraging the little boy inside, restating my reasons for quitting, and looking forward to the new life that was waiting for me if I could just keep myself under control.

A really simple method that you can use to snap yourself back into reality is called the rubber band technique. Have you ever watched the Dog Whisperer, Cesar Milan? When he's training a dog to walk on a lead without barking or trying to attack other dogs or people, he uses a technique that snaps the dog out of its aggressive behavior pattern, before the behavior can escalate. When he notices his dog looking in the direction of another dog with an intention of fighting, he will use his foot to gently tap the dog in its hind area, between the belly and the top of its back leg. This snaps the dog's attention away from what it was focusing on, preventing an escalation.

Here's how the rubber band technique works.

What to Do

1. Take a rubber band and put it over your wrist. You are going to be wearing this band for a while so make sure you buy one that you're comfortable wearing. It also needs to be strong enough to snap against your skin without breaking.

2. Decide on a single sentence that you're going to say to yourself when you need to snap yourself out of the misery thinking.

For instance:

"Snap yourself out of it!"

"There is nothing wrong. It's just my anxiety trying to get the better of me."

"The discomfort will pass."

"There you are again, critical thought. I'm still not going to entertain you. You might as well stop trying."

3. The trick is to snap the rubber band three times when you think a thought that makes you feel stressed, when you feel yourself in glorified moaning posture. Snapping the band will only sting a little, that's good! You need the reminder. Then say your mantra out loud with every snap.

4. Just repeat as needed.

Why does it work?

As in the example of the Dog Whisperer, this technique works because it brings your attention to your glorified moaning and prevents it from escalating. You're never going to stop the thoughts from happening, that's impossible. All you can do is become more aware that they are happening, accept them as a normal part of you as a healthy, fully-functioning human being, deal with them quickly, and move on.

79. Taking a Glimpse into Infinity

Fractal watching is another very strange, yet calming method of destressing. Looking at fractals is a bit like watching a log fire or fish swimming around in an aquarium. There's something in a fractal that attracts our eye and excites the relaxation responses deep within our brains.

A fractal is a continuous and never-ending pattern. The self-similar pattern repeats itself regardless of which range you view it. As you zoom in, the pattern keeps repeating. There's many examples of fractals in nature - snowflakes, leaves, flowers, and the art world is also full of its own examples. Jackson Pollock is one famous artist who has used this type of patterning to great effect.

Research has shown that patterns, whether they come from fractals, the consistency sound from ocean waves, snowflakes, or patterns in a fire, have a calming effect on the nervous system. Physicist Richard Taylor of the University of Oregon says, "People are 'hard-wired' to respond to a specific form of fractal found in nature, one that reduces stress levels by up to 60%. This stress-reduction is triggered by a physiological resonance that occurs when the fractal structure of the eye matches that of the fractal image being viewed."

What to Do

1. Simply go for a walk and commune with nature. Visit a local park, a botanical gardens, or just sit in a quiet spot staring at the clouds.

2. Buy some fractal art for your home or workplace. You don't

have to spend hours staring at a picture on the wall, just the presence of more fractals in your environment can result in a calming effect.

80. To Change Your Life, First Change Your Mind

Most people associate hypnosis with some sort of higgery jiggery or with a slick manipulator who can make people squawk like chickens. In fact, nobody can be hypnotized without their awareness and permission. However, hypnosis can help you, whether that be through a trained hypnotist or through your own efforts.

We're going to look at a few ways you can help yourself through self-hypnosis. The form of self-hypnosis I'll be writing about here is self-guided mental imagery.

Mental imagery is a technique for stress management, to bring about a relaxed state by using your memory and imagination to conjure up peaceful, relaxing scenes in your mind. It's up to you what type of images you think about. The idea is to recall, recreate, or create a scene that helps you to relax. Guided imagery is a form of self-hypnosis that can also be used to create and achieve the goals you want in life and to build a healthy self-image. So it's a powerful all-round tool.

What to Do

1. Find a quiet place where you are unlikely to be disturbed. Alternatively, if you only have a few minutes during your lunch break, a park bench will do or just sitting under a shady tree.

2. Sit or lie in a comfortable position.

3. Close your eyes.

4. Choose your guided imagination setting. Where do you

want to go? Choose a setting that's peaceful, one that has some personal meaning to you. It must be a setting which you associate with complete relaxation. It can be a real place from your memory or a place you've just imagined.

5. If you can't think of any place, here are some suggestions:

A. You're in a log cabin in the mountains. Outside it's snowing, but inside is warm and dry. You sit in front of a roaring log fire, a cup of cocoa in your hands. Listen to the crackling of the fire. Feel the heat from the fire radiating out over your body and face. Feel and taste the warm cocoa as you drink from the cup. Watch the snow as it falls gently past one of the windows. Enjoy the happiness you are experiencing right now.

B. You are lying on a sunny beach, somewhere far from your daily life. You feel the soft, warm sand beneath your body, between your fingers and toes. You hear the breeze rippling through the palm trees, shading you from the sun. Listen to the gentle lapping waters as the waves swish back and forth across the beach. Feel the warm, soft air gently brushing over your body. You feel relaxed and comfortable, no stress.

C. You are sitting with your friends and family in a lush green meadow, under the shade of a mighty oak tree. You feel the sun's warmth overhead, the grass beneath you, and you are really enjoying the voices and laughter of the people around you.

6. As you can see from the above examples, the more senses you can bring into your imagery, the more realistic your mental imagery will be.

7. Don't bring anything negative into your visualizations. If you feel negative thoughts intruding into your scene, acknowledge them and then release them, replacing them with only positive and relaxed thoughts.

8. Expect to feel your body and mind relaxing, remember that your expectations are half the battle. Take deep breathes.

9. If you find that there's sounds or smells from your real environment intruding into your fantasy, incorporate them within

your visualization.

 10. Relax and enjoy.

81. Worshiping in the Summer Sun

"Our ancestors worshiped the Sun, and they were not that foolish. It makes sense to revere the Sun and the stars, for we are their children."

Carl Sagan

When I look at our sun, even when it's beating down on my head on a hot Spanish summer's day, I'm in awe. Without it we're screwed. Watching the sun come up in the morning is a much more spiritual experience for me than I've ever found within the walls of any church. There's just something very primal about it, the new day dawning. The same goes for the sunset, saying goodbye to the old day, resting and recuperating during the night hours, and beginning afresh the next morning.

American stand-up comedian, George Carlin said, "Sun worship is fairly simple. There's no mystery, no miracles, no pageantry, no one asks for money, there are no songs to learn, and we don't have a special building where we all gather once a week to compare our clothing." See the rest of this funny routine here: https://www.youtube.com/watch?v=B4diugMg5kQ

Apart from this basic human awe that I feel for the daily movement of our planet across the face of our nearest star, there's also the essential life-giving nature that the sun provides for us, everything we know on this planet is impossible without the sun. In terms of getting out there and enjoying the sunshine, it helps to release our feel-good chemicals. Serotonin is a natural chemical produced by the body which regulates mood, sleep, appetite, and memory. Another chemical associated with our beneficent sun is melatonin. A study by the Baker Heart Research Institute in Melbourne found that lower levels of serotonin had a direct correlation with seasonal affective disorder (SAD). SAD most often occurs during the bleak winter months when people are not getting enough sun.

But aren't we told to stay out of the sun? Humans have been on this planet for millions of years. We evolved through those millions of years with the same sun over our heads, yet it's only in the last 50 to 100 years that the problems of sun exposure have been highlighted. In fact, skin cancer rates have soared in the last 50 years. Why is that? Sun worshiping, throwing caution to the wind and basking in the sun from dawn until dusk is not advisable. But you shouldn't be afraid to expose yourself to the sun's rays. You need it, and the benefits far outweigh the risks.

What to Do

1. 10 to 15 minutes sun exposure is all you need to get your supply of vitamin D for the day.

2. You don't have to sit directly in the sun, find a shaded spot and just enjoy being outdoors.

3. At the hottest times of the day, stay in the shade or wear hats and clothing to cover your skin.

4. Never over-expose yourself to the sun.

What Now?

Welcome to the final section of Hang Loose Without Booze. Thank you for sticking it out until the end and I really hope you found some new pathways that will lead you to a more relaxed life.

The suggestions I have made in this book are only that, suggestions. Part of the problem of quitting is replacing the alcohol and the time spent drinking and recovering from the poisoning with more beneficial activities. What I've outlined in this book is just the tip of the iceberg. There's a whole world out there to explore, a lot of it on your own doorstep, or even better, in your own mind.

Like many people in the same situation, I used to have a one-track mind when it came to entertainment. If it didn't involve alcohol, it wasn't very bloody entertaining! It took a while, but I've developed a whole new way of looking at life, relaxing, de-stressing, and having fun. Most of it comes from in my head.

It's easy to stop drinking, you can do it in a single moment. One minute you're a drinker, the next you're not. Let's face it, you've got to physically put the stuff in your mouth for you to continue drinking it. So it's not a question of can't, it's a question of won't.

How much do you want to stop versus how much do you want to continue?

How much do you want to carry on down this easy street that you've been taking, even though easy street is killing you slowly?

How much time and energy are you willing to invest in your own life in finding your better way? - Your better way of relaxation, your better way of dealing with stress, problems, personal issues, all those things in your life that you've been turning to alcohol to solve?

So it's not really about not drinking alcohol any more. You already know that you can do that. If you were locked in a room with no alcohol, you wouldn't be able to drink it. You'd be forced to quit. You might feel crap for a while, you might think that the world was going to come to an end, you might believe that not drinking alcohol is impossible. But at the end of the day, when you can't drink, you won't drink. You won't fall apart or drop dead. You'll get used to it. This proves that alcohol drinking is a habit that can be easily broken when you can't do it anymore, when you're not in a position to do it anymore. So you know that lifting that glass to your lips, taking the contents into your mouth, and swallowing each and every mouthful is completely down to your decision to do it.

So the question is not how to not put the drink in your body any more, that's simple! The real question is do you want to not put the alcohol into your body anymore and how much do you really want this?

Unless you possess rock hard motivation to do this from the start, and this motivation is going to carry you through any amount of temptation that you might face along the way, you're going to find yourself facing these types of questions eventually.

These questions might come up for you after you've only done a day. It might be after a couple of days, once the hangover illness has worn off. You might start to ask yourself these things after a couple of months into your new life, as the novelty of your new found self is wearing thin. You feel great, you look great, you think great, but you feel like you're missing out on something.

As I said, it is simple to stop the flow, but it's not that simple to switch off your automatic longing for alcohol, the brainwashing that's been built up over a lifetime. Although alcohol is really a very ineffective tool for your long term health and happiness, we tend not to think about our lives in that way. We mostly think about our feelings and emotions in the moment, how we feel right now, what affects us right now, or what are we motivated to do right now.

When you do drugs, whether that drug is heroin or alcohol, you have at your disposal an instant fix to all your life's problems. Take the drug and you don't have to think about your problems. You don't have to worry. You get peace and quiet from the nagging voice within your head. Job done. At least for a while.

But of course, you know that taking a drug is not a real solution to any of your problems. Dealing with life through drug use is only a facade, a pretense of the highest order. Every long-term drinker knows that the only person they're kidding is themselves. Unfortunately, we can easily hide from that realization as well. You don't have to think about these things when you're out of it on a drug. You don't have to give a damn about anything else but what's happening in that moment because you're under the influence, high as a kite, drunk. You can kick the habit tomorrow. You can deal with your problems tomorrow. You can think about it tomorrow.

Life doesn't work that way. Every time you force these delay tactics on yourself, you change the way you see yourself. You change your self-perception a tiny bit towards viewing yourself as a quitter, a procrastinator, a scaredy cat. Do you follow?

That's why you need to focus your attention on finding new ways of achieving the same ends that you've been getting from the booze. New ways of relaxation, new ways of relieving your stress, new ways of dealing with your problems.

None of us are stupid. We know that not dealing with a problem doesn't make the problem go away. We understand from our own experiences that things tend to get worse when we procrastinate, when we continuously put things off until tomorrow.

Quitting drinking is immediate. Dealing with the pull from your mates to go to the pub, the call of the habitual beer at night while you watch the TV, the so-called normal drinking that everyone else seems to be able to do, except you, which leads to the feelings that there's something wrong with you... these are all things you have to deal with in the long-term. And they're tough!

These are all the things you have to deal with one you refuse to hide behind the bottle. When you take your head out of the sand and start to look at life on its own merits, you realize that everything you need is already there. To get to those things you have to go through a process of discovery. And it's a gradual process.

It's a gradual process of finding new things to do with your time, new drinks to drink, and new ways of thinking. As the days pass, and your body and mind heals, you will know intuitively that what you've just done was the right thing for you to do, it was the right decision to make. You'll know that there is nothing wrong with you. You're not a freak, you're not abnormal, and you're not an alcoholic.

If you persevere with this, if you are diligent in seeking out those better alternatives for yourself, alternatives that will plug into YOUR life, you will never look back. You will never want to drink alcohol again. You will never want to take any drug ever again.

You'll feel more in control of yourself than you have ever felt before. More in control of your life than you have ever felt before. You will feel more optimistic about the journey that's waiting ahead of you. You will extend the length of your life, but more importantly the quality of your life. You'll also be a great influence in giving that gift to those around you.

I'm not exaggerating when I say that through your decision to quit taking this drug, you're going to inspire many people in your life. You may be just the person that these people have been waiting for, a leader, someone who's got it right, someone who they can follow, who they can look up to. Sometimes, all it takes is for one person to change, showing that it can be done.

Finding new ways of doing things, new ways of living your life, of truly living your life, is just a process. It's no more than a set of skills that you need to learn.

It's the same process you will need to go through when you're trying to find alternatives to going to the pub, drinking to relax, to have fun, to celebrate, and all the other things you've been using the alcoholic hammer for. But instead of relying on this one inefficient, toxic, dangerous tool, you'll find there's a whole world of more appropriate, beneficial, rewarding, and fulfilling opportunities waiting for you. They were there all the time, you just couldn't see them because your mind was narrowly focused on one form of doing things... drinking alcohol.

The material that I've talked about in *Hang Loose Without Booze* is just the tip of the iceberg. It's a big world out there with plenty of opportunities to have fun and enjoy yourself. Relaxation and stress relief doesn't have to cost a fortune. You don't have to book a week long session into a spa, spend a fortune jetting off to a tropical island, nor do you need to take head-therapy for the rest of your life. It would be nice to have some of these things, but they're not very helpful in your day to day life.

The most beneficial skills for you to learn are those which are cheap, or free, take only a small investment of time and energy before you see some results, can be practiced without having to travel, and can be easily built into your life.

Relaxation and stress management is about taking care of yourself in the here and now so that the long term takes care of itself. If you learn to relax and manage your stress without the aid of drugs, you give yourself a priceless gift.

The simple tools that I've laid out here will help you to do just that. When you feel yourself getting wound up, you know what to do. Dig into your personal arsenal of stress-busting skillsets and choose the right one for you in that moment.

Whether you use any of the suggestion in *Hang Loose Without Booze* is up to you. I hope at the very least you get some ideas for your own simple, easy-to-implement, relaxation builders and stress busters.

Until next time, I'm Kevin O'Hara for AlcoholMastery.com...

Onwards and Upwards!

AlcoholMastery.com

Come to AlcoholMastery.com where you'll find a ton of helpful videos for quitting the booze.

Other Books by Kevin O'Hara

How to Stop Drinking Alcohol - A Simple Path From Alcohol Misery To Alcohol Mastery

Alcohol Freedom - 7 Powerful Mindsets to Kickstart Your Alcohol-Free Journey!

58031744R00119

Made in the USA
Lexington, KY
30 November 2016